walkernaths 2.13 SIMULATIONS

NCEA Level 2 Internal

Charlotte Walker and Victoria Walker

Australia • Brazil • Mexico • Singapore • United Kingdom • United States

Walker Maths 2.13 Simulations
1st Edition
Charlotte Walker
Victoria Walker

Designer: Cheryl Smith, Macarn Design
Production controller: Alice Kane

Any URLs contained in this publication were checked for currency during the production process. Note, however, that the publisher cannot vouch for the ongoing currency of URLs.

Acknowledgements
Cover photo courtesy of iStock.

We wish to thank the Boards of Trustees of Darfield and Riccarton High Schools for allowing us to use materials and ideas developed while teaching. Our thanks also go to all past and present colleagues, especially Kath Wilson, who have generously shared their experience and ideas.

For product information and technology assistance,
in Australia call **1300 790 853**;
in New Zealand call **0800 449 725**

For permission to use material from this text or product, please email **aust.permissions@cengage.com**

National Library of New Zealand Cataloguing-in-Publication Data
A catalogue record for this book is available from the National Library of New Zealand.

978 0 17 041599 6

Cengage Learning Australia
Level 7, 80 Dorcas Street
South Melbourne, Victoria Australia 3205

Cengage Learning New Zealand
Unit 4B Rosedale Office Park
331 Rosedale Road, Albany, North Shore 0632, NZ

For learning solutions, visit **cengage.co.nz**

Printed in China by 1010 Printing International Limited
9 25

CONTENTS

ISBN: 9780170415996

Glossary

Make your own glossary of key terms:

Term	Definition	Picture/Example
Simulation		
Random		
Frequency		
Trial		
Outcome		
Independent		

What is a simulation?

- To simulate means to pretend, to imitate, to mimic.
- In a simulation we imitate a probability situation using devices such as cards, random numbers, dice, coins, etc.

The purpose of a simulation: To estimate a probability or expected value in situations when:

- a precise mathematical model is not available to calculate the probability or expected value
- applying a mathematical model is difficult, time consuming or expensive.

For a simulation to produce accurate results:

1 The model on which the simulation is based must accurately reflect the real situation.
2 The simulation must be repeated many times.

ISBN: 9780170415996

In this standard you will need to:

1 Decide what device (dice, cards, random numbers, etc.) you will use.

2 Describe how you will use your selected device.

3 Define what one trial will be.

4 State how many trials you will do.

5 Carry out the simulation and record the results in a table.

6 Show calculations resulting from the outcome: usually an expected value or a probability.

7 Communicate your findings in a conclusion.

8 Discuss your results and any assumptions made.

Probability revision

The range of values for probabilities

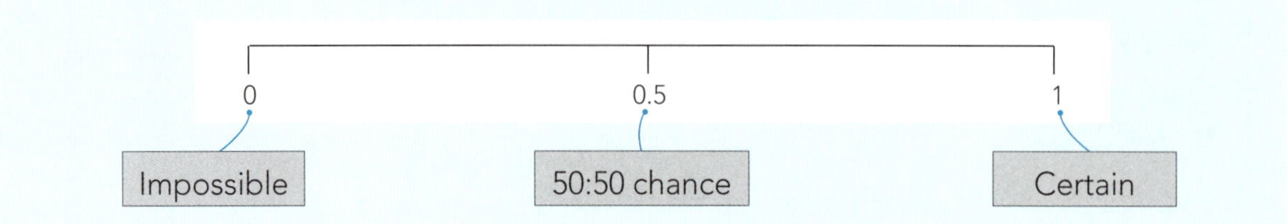

Using numbers to write probabilities

- Probabilities can be written as **fractions**, **decimals** or **percentages**.
- You can convert between these with your calculator.
- When you want to compare probabilities, it is often easiest to use **decimals**.
- Round decimal probability values to a maximum of 4 dp.

Example: Write the probability $\frac{5}{13}$ as a decimal: 5 [÷] 13 [=] 0.3846

Convert the following probabilities to decimals, and state which of each pair is more likely.

1 $\frac{4}{13}$ = ________ $\frac{1}{3}$ = ________

More likely: ________

2 $\frac{3}{4}$ = ________ $\frac{10}{13}$ = ________

More likely: ________

3 $\frac{1}{18}$ = ________ $\frac{3}{57}$ = ________

More likely: ________

4 $\frac{6}{17}$ = ________ $\frac{4}{11}$ = ________

More likely: ________

Match the following probabilities to the words which would best describe them.
Hint: Convert all of them to decimals first.

5 $\frac{7}{14989}$ ________

6 $\frac{8}{17}$ ________

7 $\frac{23}{32}$ ________

8 0.9421 ________

9 $\frac{89}{90}$ ________

10 0.0643 ________

Very likely
Maybe
Slight chance
Highly unlikely
Probable
Almost certain

 ISBN: 9780170415996

Ways of calculating probabilities

1 Equally likely outcomes

$$\textbf{Probability} = \frac{\textbf{number of favourable outcomes}}{\textbf{total possible outcomes}}$$

Remember: The **sum** of all the probabilities for an event must **add to 1**.

Example 1: For a fair die, P(1, 2, 3 or a 4) = $\frac{4}{6}$ or $\frac{2}{3}$ or $0.\dot{6}$

Example 2: Using a pack of cards with no jokers (52 cards):

P(king of diamonds) = $\frac{1}{52}$ or 0.0192

P(diamond) = $\frac{13}{52}$ or $\frac{1}{4}$ or 0.25

P(king) = $\frac{4}{52}$ or $\frac{1}{13}$ or 0.0769

P(king or a diamond) = $\frac{16}{52}$ or 0.3077

Calculate the following probabilities.

When tossing a fair die:

1 P(1) = ____________

2 P(1 or 2) = ____________

3 P(4, 5 or 6) = ____________

4 P(not a 5) = ____________

5 P(0) = ____________

6 P(1, 2, 3, 4, 5 or 6) = ____________

Using a pack of cards with no jokers (52 cards), and selecting one card at random:

7 P(spade) = ____________

8 P(red card) = ____________

9 P(3) = ____________

10 P(red jack) = ____________

11 P(ace or 2) = ____________

12 P(red 2, black 5 or an 8) = ____________

13 P(a red card or an ace) = ____________

14 P(neither a jack nor a king) = ____________

Sugarfix cereal puts a plastic vehicle in each box: 10% of boxes contain a car, 30% of boxes contain a truck, 40% of boxes contain a motor bike, and the rest of the boxes contain buses.

15 P(a bus) = ____________

16 P(not getting a truck) = ____________

17 P(a bus or a truck) = ____________

18 P(getting neither a car nor a bus) = ____________

ISBN: 9780170415996

2 Long run relative frequency

- The 'long run' may refer to the recording of events over a long period of time, e.g. calculating the probability of an earthquake greater than 8 on the Richter scale in a ten-year period would involve counting the number of earthquakes over hundreds or thousands of years.
- It may refer to the recording of events over a short period, e.g. calculating the probability of an irregular heartbeat in one minute could involve recording heartbeats over 30 minutes.
- It may involve the recording of many events at the same time, e.g. calculating the probability that an NCEA candidate will get Merit in an external exam involves recording the results of events that happen simultaneously.
- Unless we can collect data for the whole population, the **true value** of the probability will **never be known**.
- **The greater the number of trials, the closer our estimate for the probability will be to the true probability.**

$$\textbf{Probability} = \frac{\textbf{number of favourable outcomes}}{\textbf{total possible outcomes}}$$

Example: There were 280 students at the senior formal. Of these, 203 were driven there by parents, 24 drove themselves, 32 were driven by friends, 19 walked and 2 people rode their bicycles.

P(a student drove themselves to the formal) $= \frac{\text{number of students who drove themselves to the formal}}{\text{total number of students attending the formal}}$

$$= \frac{24}{280} = 0.0857$$

P(a student arrived at the formal in a vehicle) $= \frac{\text{number of students who arrived at the formal in a vehicle}}{\text{total number of students attending the formal}}$

$$= \frac{203 + 24 + 32}{280} = 0.925$$

P(a student did not walk to the formal) $= \frac{\text{number of students who did not walk to the formal}}{\text{total number of students attending the formal}}$

$$= \frac{280 - 19}{280} = 0.9321$$

Calculate the following probabilities.

1 Of the 280 students at the senior formal, 96 came with partners from within the school, 37 brought partners from other schools, and 147 came with groups of friends.

a Calculate the probability that a student came with a partner from within the school.

____

b Calculate the probability that a student came with a partner.

____

 ISBN: 9780170415996

2 There are 29 students in a class. In the simulations assessment, 11 students got Excellence grades, 10 got Merit, 7 got Achieved grades, and 1 got Not Achieved.

a Calculate the probability that a student got an Excellence grade.

____

b Calculate the probability that a student got neither a Merit nor an Excellence grade.

____

3 Megan threw two dice and subtracted the smaller score from the bigger one. She did this 50 times and got the following results.

Difference	**0**	**1**	**2**	**3**	**4**	**5**
Frequency	8	14	11	6	7	4

a Calculate the probability that the difference between the two dice was 4.

____

b Calculate the probability that the difference between the dice was less than 3.

____

4 Old dice were sometimes weighted by gamblers. This often involved inserting a tiny ball of lead into one side or corner so that some numbers were more likely to occur than others. This meant that all outcomes were not equally likely.
It is suspected that a die has been weighted. It was tossed 34 times, and the results are shown in the table.

Number tossed	**1**	**2**	**3**	**4**	**5**	**6**
Frequency	3	3	5	8	9	6

a Calculate the probabilities of the following events using the suspect die, and compare them with those for a fair die.

	Suspect die	**Fair die**
P(1)		
P(1 or 2)		
P(4, 5 or 6)		
P(not a 5)		

b These probabilities suggest that the suspect die might be weighted. Describe what you could do in order to be more certain of this conclusion.

____

____

ISBN: 9780170415996

Expected number of outcomes

Expected number of outcomes = P(event) x number of trials

Example 1: A die was thrown 180 times. Calculate the expected number of times a 5 or a 6 is thrown.

$$\begin{aligned}\text{Expected number of 5s or 6s} &= P(5 \text{ or } 6) \times 180 \\ &= 0.\dot{3} \times 180 \\ &= 60\end{aligned}$$

Example 2: The probability that a left-handed person in Great Britain dies as a result of using a right-handed product (e.g. scissors) is $\frac{1}{4,400,000}$ in one year. If in 2018 the population of Great Britain is 66 573 500, calculate the expected number of left-handed people who will die as a result of using a right-handed product in Great Britain during 2018.

$$\begin{aligned}\text{Expected number of people} &= \frac{1}{4,400,000} \times 66\,573\,500 \\ &= 15 \text{ or } 16\end{aligned}$$

The exact answer is 15.1303…, but this is people, so we must round to the nearest whole person.

Answer the following questions.

1 A die was thrown 54 times. Calculate the expected number of throws that would produce a number greater than 4.

2 A card was drawn from a 52-card pack; its identity was recorded and it was replaced in the pack. This was repeated 100 times. Calculate the expected number of picture cards (jacks, queens or kings).

3 The probability that a baby will be born with dextrocardia (the heart on the right side of the body instead of the left) is 0.0000832. In 2017, there were 59 430 babies born in New Zealand. How many of these would you expect to be born with dextrocardia?

4 The probability that a person dreams in colour is 0.95. How many students at a school with a role of 878 would you expect to dream in black and white only?

5 In the game of poker, each player is dealt a hand of five cards. The probability that a hand contains just three of a kind (three aces, three kings, etc.) is 0.2113 and the probability of getting four of a kind is 0.00024. If 94 hands are dealt during the course of a game, how many of these would be expected to contain three or four of a kind?

ISBN: 9780170415996

Mixing it up

Answer the following questions.

1 Of the cells in the human body, red blood cells make up 8.4% and other human cells make up 1.8%. The remainder are bacterial cells. If a body cell is chosen at random, what is the probability it is a bacterial cell?

2 The number of babies born in New Zealand during 2017 was 59 430. The probability that a baby is born with 11 fingers or toes is 0.002. Calculate the expected number of babies born in New Zealand during 2017 with 11 fingers or toes.

3 A vet treats 15 animals during his morning surgery. There were 7 dogs, 4 cats, 2 guinea pigs, a rat and a tortoise.

a Calculate the probability that his first patient in the morning was a dog.

b Calculate the probability that his first patient in the morning is not a cat.

c Calculate the probability that his first patient in the morning was neither a cat nor a dog.

4 A manufacturer of TV remote controllers has discovered that if you have lost one, the probability that it is lost between your sofa cushions is 0.5, the probability that it is in the fridge or the freezer is 0.04 and the probability that it is outside or in the car is 0.02. Calculate the probability that it is not in any of these places.

5 Just 30% of people can flare their nostrils. If your school roll is 687, how many students would you expect to be able to flare their nostrils?

6 Rip-off Repairs give away a packet of jelly beans with every car repair they do. Each packet contains 17 jelly beans. In each packet, eight are black, five are red and four are white. Jackson has a packet and closes his eyes while he picks each jelly bean.

a Calculate the probability that the first jelly bean he picks is not white.

b If it was white and he ate it, calculate the probability that the second jelly bean he picks is black or white.

ISBN: 9780170415996

Randomness and independence

- Random means **not able to be predicted, having no pattern**.
- Randomness in probability means that events are **independent** of each other: a previous outcome does not affect the probability that an event will occur.
- In simulations, it is very important that we use **independent random events** to simulate what is happening in reality.

Independence

Example of events that are independent:
The events 'a student is a boy' and 'a student plays sport' are independent if boys and girls are equally likely to play a sport.

Example of events that are not independent:
The events 'a student is a boy' and 'a student plays netball' are not independent if boys are less likely to play netball than girls.

Decide whether the following events are **likely** to be independent or not:

	Events		Independent or not independent?
1	A school student is in Year 13.	The school student is attempting Level 3 standards.	
2	A Year 12 student studies mathematics.	The Year 12 student buys their lunch from the canteen.	
3	A student skips assembly.	The student is in Year 11, 12 or 13.	
4	A phone belongs to a student.	The phone is the latest iPhone.	
5	A person plays bowls.	The person is over 60 years old.	
6	A car is grey.	The car is worth more than $10 000.	
7	A car is a Mercedes.	The car is worth more than $10 000.	
8	Throwing a die five times and getting the numbers 1, 2, 3, 4 and 5.	Getting a 6 on the next throw.	
9	Tossing a coin ten times and getting ten heads.	Tossing a coin again and getting a head.	

ISBN: 9780170415996

Devices that can be used to produce independent random events:

1 **Dice:** We assume that the die used in a simulation is **fair**. That means that every throw of the die is equally likely to produce a 1, 2, 3, 4, 5 or 6.

2 **Playing cards (52-card pack):** Every time a card is drawn from a shuffled pack (with replacement), it is equally likely to be any card in the pack.

Note: If the drawn card is **not** replaced, then drawing cards is **no longer independent**.

For the first card: $P(\text{ace}) = \frac{4}{52} = 0.0769$

When a second card is drawn, the probability of getting an ace depends on the outcome of the first draw:

If the first card was an ace, then: $P(\text{ace}) = \frac{3}{51} = 0.0588$

If the first card was not an ace: $P(\text{ace}) = \frac{4}{51} = 0.0784$

These probabilities are different from each other ⇒ events are **not** independent.

3 **Random numbers:** Random numbers can be obtained in a number of ways such as:

- drawing numbers from a hat (with replacement)
- using a computer program
- using a scientific calculator
- using a graphics calculator.

Note: In Lotto they use a rotating barrel containing numbered balls which are not replaced, because numbers cannot be repeated. This means that the probability that (say) ball 40 is drawn depends on what has happened in previous draws.

For the first ball, $P(40) = \frac{1}{40} = 0.025$.

For the second ball;

If the first ball was 40, then $P(40) = 0$.

If the first ball was not a 40, then $P(40) = \frac{1}{39} = 0.02564$.

So while the draw is random, the probabilities that any particular ball is drawn are not independent.

4 **Spinners:** In theory you could use a spinner, but in practice, constructing one that is truly random is very difficult.

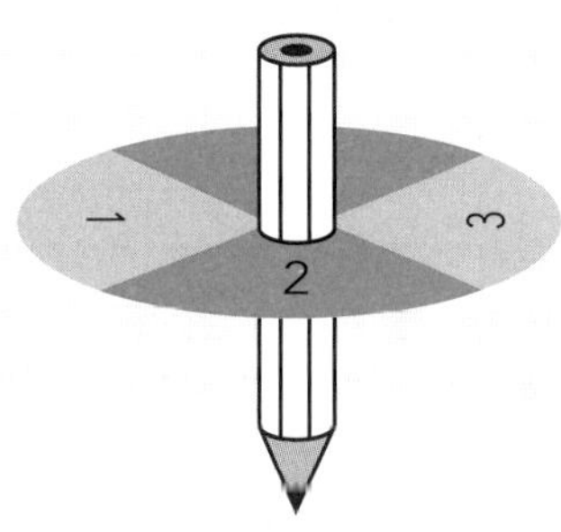

ISBN: 9780170415996

Finding random numbers on a scientific calculator

Step 1: Find the RAN or RAN# button.

Try pressing the = button. You will get a four-digit number between 0.001 and 0.999. You can use the digits after the decimal points as your random numbers, but it is easier if you follow **steps 2** and **3** below.

Note: If you use the four-digit numbers, beware numbers with fewer digits — your calculator will have left off the final zeros.

Step 2: If you need 8 random numbers ranging from 1 to 6, enter:

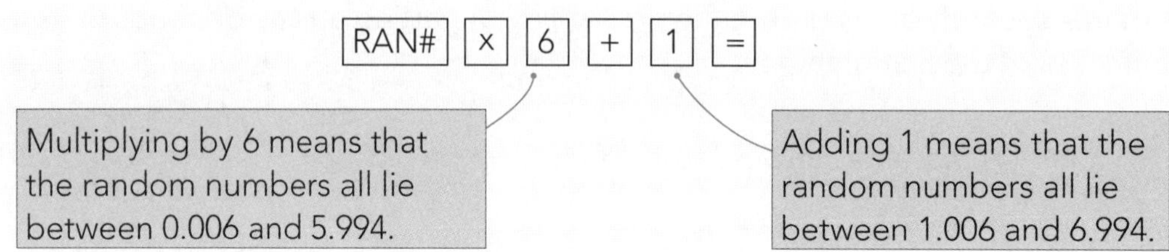

Step 3: Press = 8 times.

Example of results:

Use the digit **before** the decimal point as your random number (do not round).

On calculator	5.464	6.034	1.864	1.64	2.626	3.364	2.278	6.832
Random number	5	6	1	1	2	3	2	6

Another example:

Step 2: If you need 7 random numbers ranging from 1 to 58, enter:

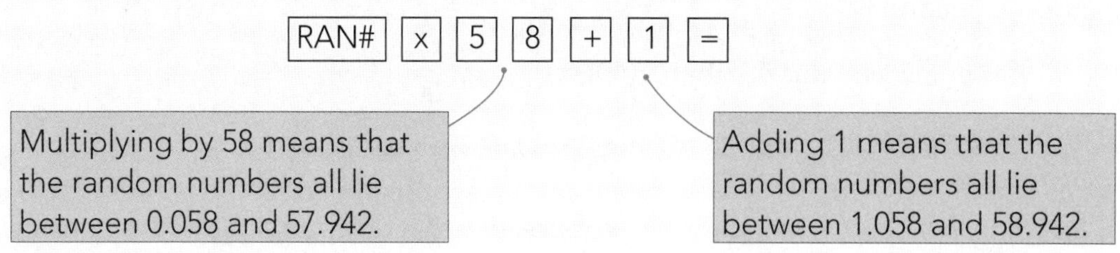

Step 3: Press = 7 times.

Example of results:

On calculator	36.496	21.996	12.832	11.15	36.438	54.824	7.728
Random numbers	36	21	12	11	36	54	7

ISBN: 9780170415996

Finding random numbers on a graphics calculator

Step 1:
⇒ RUN
⇒ EXE
⇒ OPTN
⇒ F6 ▷
⇒ F3 PROB
⇒ F4 RAND
⇒ F2 Int

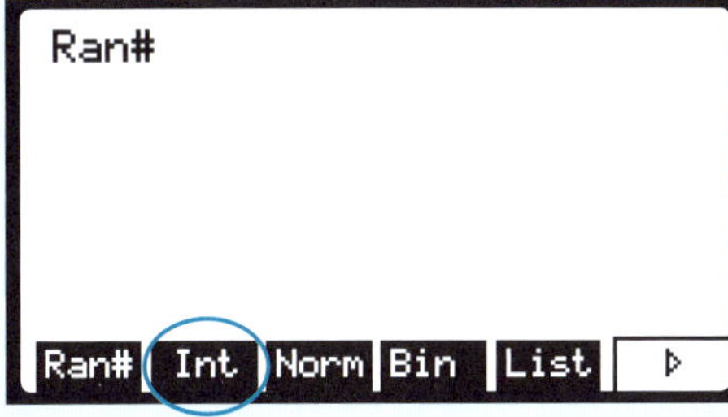

Step 2: If you need 4 random numbers ranging from 1 to 150, enter:

If you have an older graphics calculator, follow the first five instructions from above and then enter:

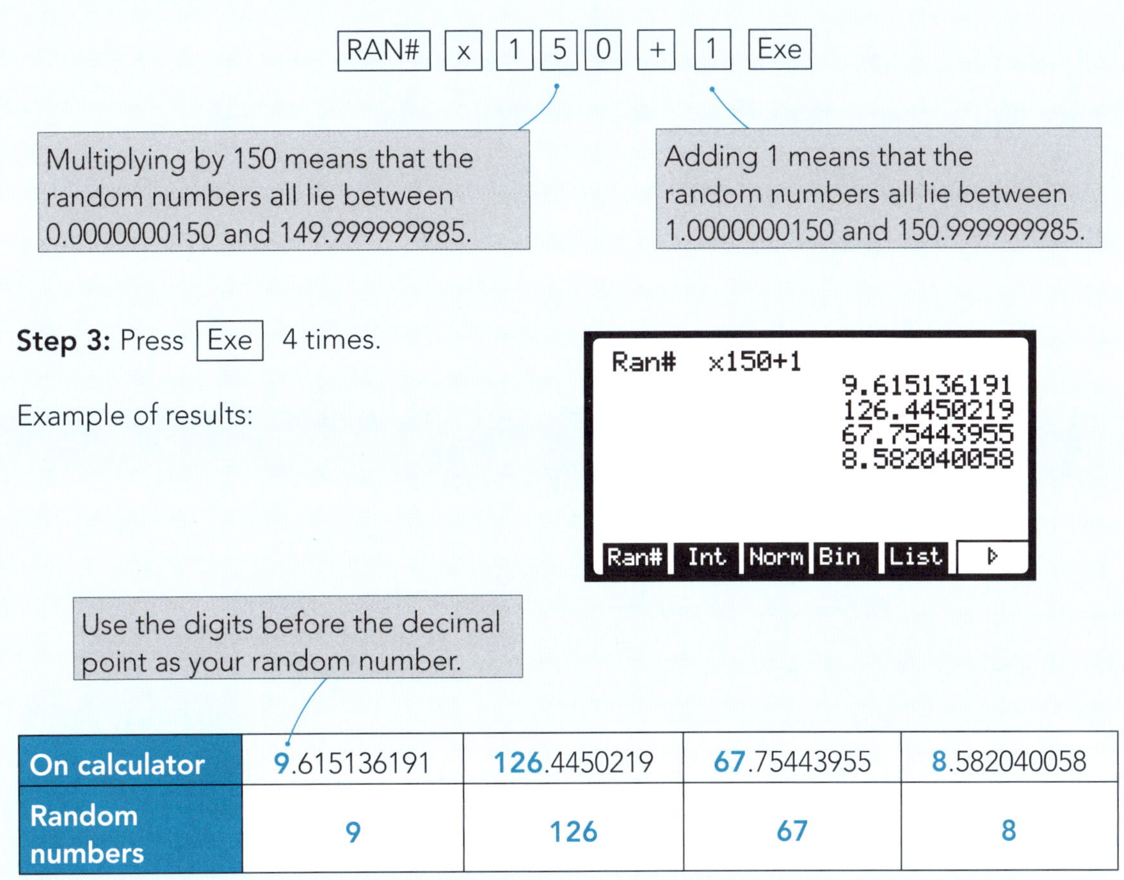

Step 3: Press Exe 4 times.

Example of results:

On calculator	9.615136191	126.4450219	67.75443955	8.582040058
Random numbers	9	126	67	8

Note: In practice you will be finding many more random numbers than in these examples.

ISBN: 9780170415996

Some situations suitable for simulation

Think about each of these situations, discuss them with others in your class and then estimate the probabilities below.

Example 1: A soft drink promotion involves collecting bottle caps which have one of the following letters printed on the inside: S, N, A, P. Amy bought a bottle each day from the school canteen. The soft drink company has distributed caps with the following probabilities for each letter:

Letter	S	N	A	P
Probability	0.4	0.3	0.2	0.1

a Estimate the number of bottle caps Amy needs in order to complete the word 'SNAP'.

My estimate of the number of caps needed to complete the word 'SNAP' = ___________

b Estimate the probability that she completes the word 'SNAP' with 12 caps or fewer.

My estimate of the probability that she completes the word 'SNAP' with 12 caps or fewer

= ___________

Example 2: A farmer has a small flock of sheep and knows the following probabilities:

Probability (ewe produces a single lamb) = 0.49
Probability (ewe produces twins) = 0.45
Probability (ewe produces triplets) = 0.06

The farmer retires his ewes from breeding after a ewe produces single lambs for two years in a row, or after six years of breeding, whichever comes first.

a Estimate the mean number of years that he allows each ewe to breed.

My estimate of the mean number of years that he allows each ewe to breed = ___________

b Estimate the probability that a ewe is allowed to breed for six years.

My estimate of the probability that a ewe is allowed to breed for six years = ___________

c Estimate the probability that a ewe has triplets during her breeding life.

My estimate of the probability that a ewe has triplets during her breeding life

= ___________

 ISBN: 9780170415996

The simulation process

1 Using a device to simulate probabilities

Step 1: Make sure that you:
- know what all the possible outcomes are
- know the probability of each outcome
- check that all these probabilities add to 1.

Step 2: Decide which device you will use.

Step 3: Describe how you will use your device.

Step 4: Create a table showing:

Every possible outcome				
Probability of each outcome				
Random numbers, numbers from dice, etc.				

Which results from your device will represent each outcome.

Example 1: A soft drink promotion involves collecting bottle caps which have one of the following letters printed on the inside: S, N, A, P. Amy bought a bottle each day from the school canteen. The soft drink company has distributed caps with the following probabilities for each letter:

Letter	S	N	A	P
Probability	0.4	0.3	0.2	0.1

Step 1: *Probabilities = 0.4 + 0.3 + 0.2 + 0.1 = 1*

Step 2: *The device I will use is a pack of playing cards.*

Step 3: *This is how I will use my pack of playing cards:*
- *I will draw cards from a 52-card pack, replacing each card after it has been drawn.*
- *I will record only the aces and the numbers 2 to 10.*
- *I will ignore the picture cards (jack, queen and king).*
- *This means that the probability for getting each of the ace and numbers 2 to 10 is 0.1.*

Step 4:

Every possible outcome	S	N	A	P
Probability of each outcome	0.4	0.3	0.2	0.1
Playing card	Ace, 2, 3, 4	5, 6, 7	8, 9	10

ISBN: 9780170415996

OR

Step 1: *Probabilities = 0.4 + 0.3 + 0.2 + 0.1 = 1*

Step 2: *The device I will use is my calculator.*

Step 3: *This is how I will use my calculator:*

- *I will use my calculator with the formula RAN x 10 + 1. I will ignore the digits after the decimal point. This will produce random numbers from 1 to 10.*
- *The probability of getting each of the numbers 1 to 10 is 0.1.*

Step 4:

Every possible outcome	S	N	A	P
Probability of each outcome	0.4	0.3	0.2	0.1
Random number	*1, 2, 3, 4*	*5, 6, 7*	*8, 9*	*10*

Example 2: A farmer has a small flock of sheep and knows the following probabilities:
Probability (sheep produces a single lamb) = 0.49
Probability (sheep produces twins) = 0.45
Probability (sheep produces triplets) = 0.06

The farmer retires his ewes from breeding after a ewe produces single lambs for two years in a row, or after six years of breeding, whichever comes first.

Using random numbers:

Step 1: *Probabilities = 0.4 + 0.3 + 0.2 + 0.1 = 1*

Step 2: *The device I will use is my calculator.*

Cards and dice would not be suitable in this situation because neither could produce probabilities of 0.01.

Step 3: *This is how I will use my calculator:*

- *I will use my calculator with the formula RAN x 100 + 1. I will ignore the digits after the decimal point. This will produce random numbers from 1 to 100.*
- *I will use the numbers 1 to 100, so the probability of getting each number is 0.01.*

Step 4:

Number of lambs	1	2	3
Probability	0.49	0.45	0.06
Random number	*1 to 49*	*50 to 94*	*95 to 100*

 ISBN: 9780170415996

Describe how you could use your chosen device to simulate probabilities in the following situations.

1 Somebody who knows nothing about the topic guesses multi-choice answers in a 14-question test where there are six possibilities for each question. Only one answer in each question is correct.

You are interested in how many questions they are likely to answer correctly, and the probability that this person will get five or more correct answers.

Step 1: ______

Step 2: ______

Step 3: ______

______

______

______

Step 4:

Outcome	Correct answer	Incorrect answer
Probability		
Number on die	1	

2 The farmer also has a flock of nine nanny goats and estimates the following probabilities:

Probability (nanny goat produces a single kid) = 0.2
Probability (nanny goat produces twins) = 0.5
Probability (nanny goat produces triplets) = 0.3

A baby goat is called a kid.

You are interested in how many kids the flock is likely to produce, and the probability that the flock produces at least 20 kids.

Step 1: ______

Step 2: ______

Step 3: ______

______

______

______

Step 4:

Number of kids			
Probability			
Random number			

ISBN: 9780170415996

3 Nick's grandmother says that she will pay Nick \$5 for every Achieved grade he gets in Mathematics, \$10 for every Merit grade and \$20 for every Excellence grade. He will be attempting five standards and he does not think he will fail any. At the start of the year, he estimates the following probabilities for his grades:

Probability (Achieved) = 0.5 Probability (Merit) = $\frac{1}{3}$ Probability (Excellence) = $\frac{1}{6}$

He is interested in how much his grandmother is likely to pay him, and the probability that she pays him at least \$50.

Grade			
Probability			
Random number			

4 The library restricts the number of books that can be borrowed to six. They found, for their customers who borrowed books, the following probabilities for the numbers of books they borrowed:

Probability (person takes out 1 book) = 0.1
Probability (person takes out 2 books) = 0.35
Probability (person takes out 3 books) = 0.25
Probability (person takes out 4 books) = 0.15
Probability (person takes out 5 books) = 0.1
Probability (person takes out 6 books) = 0.05

You are interested in the number of books in total taken out by the first 10 customers of the day, and the probability that these customers take out fewer than 30 books in total.

ISBN: 9780170415996

2 Trials

- A trial is **one performance** of a random experiment.
- In simulations it is usual to perform at least **30 trials**.
- Performing **more trials** means that you can have **greater confidence** in your results.
- You must **describe** what a **single trial** is and state how many trials you will perform.
- Give an **example** of a single trial, along with the outcomes.

Note: What your trial consists of and its outcome may vary, depending on what you are asked.

Suggested format:

One trial consists of ______________________________

until ______________________________.

I will do ________ trials.

Note: In this book only 15–30 trials have been performed, but you should do at least 30.

Example of one trial: Complete a table including at least the following:

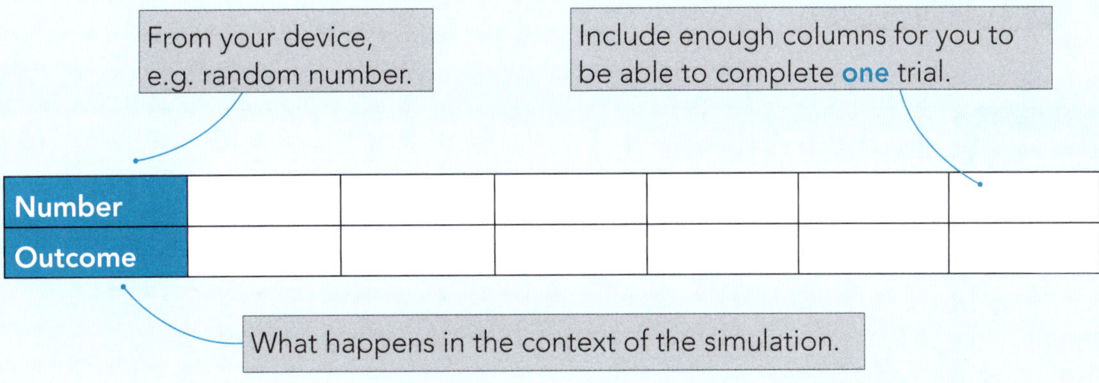

Number						
Outcome						

Trial outcome: This means that ______________________________.

Example 1: A soft drink promotion involves collecting bottle caps which have one of the following letters printed on the inside: S, N, A, P. Amy bought a bottle each day from the school canteen. The soft drink company has distributed caps with the following probabilities for each letter:

Letter	S	N	A	P
Probability	0.4	0.3	0.2	0.1

a Estimate the number of bottle caps Amy needs to complete the word 'SNAP'.

b Estimate the probability that she completes the word 'SNAP' with 12 caps or fewer.

Using playing cards: One trial consists of *drawing cards from the pack, with replacement,* ***until*** *one of each letter has been produced.*

I will do 20 trials.

Example of one trial: *I have* ***coloured*** *the first time each letter occurs.*

Every possible outcome	S	N	A	P
Probability of each outcome	0.4	0.3	0.2	0.1
Random number	*1, 2, 3, 4*	*5, 6, 7*	*8, 9*	*10*

Number	*8*	*Ace*	*2*	*3*	*8*	*7*	*9*	*6*	*7*	*9*	*2*	*8*	*8*	*9*	*10*
Letter	*A*	*S*	*S*	*S*	*A*	*N*	*A*	*N*	*N*	*A*	*S*	*A*	*A*	*A*	*P*

In this case you will have to estimate how many columns you will need, and add more if you need them.

a In this trial, how many bottle caps did Amy need in order to complete the word 'SNAP'?

Trial outcome: *This means that she needed* ***15 caps*** *to complete the word 'SNAP'.*

b Did she complete the word 'SNAP' from 12 caps or fewer in this trial?

Trial outcome: *This means that she did* ***not complete*** *the word 'SNAP' with 12 caps or fewer.*

ISBN: 9780170415996

Example 2: A farmer has a small flock of sheep and, from his lambing records, knows the following probabilities:

Probability (ewe produces a single lamb) = 0.49
Probability (ewe produces twins) = 0.45
Probability (ewe produces triplets) = 0.06

The farmer retires his ewes from breeding after a ewe produces single lambs for two years in a row, or after **six** years of breeding, whichever comes first.

a Estimate the mean number of years that he allows each ewe to breed.
b Estimate the probability that a ewe is allowed to breed for six years.
c Estimate the probability that a ewe has triplets during her breeding life.

Using random numbers: One trial consists of *finding random numbers from 1 to 100* ***until*** *two of the numbers 1 to 49 are produced consecutively, or six numbers are found.*

This would mean that the ewe has two single lambs in consecutive years.

The farmer does not allow his ewes to breed for more than six years.

I will do 20 trials.

Example of one trial:

Number of lambs	1	2	3
Probability	0.49	0.45	0.06
Random number	1 to 49	50 to 94	95 to 100

Final year of breeding because this ewe had just one lamb for two consecutive years.

In this case you will need **six** columns.

Random number	13	56	19	44	98	77
Number of lambs	1	2	1	1	3	2

a For how many years was this ewe allowed to breed?

Trial outcome: *This means that this ewe would be allowed to breed for* ***four*** *years.*

b Was the ewe allowed to breed for six years?

Trial outcome: *This means that this ewe would* ***not breed for six years****.*

c Did this ewe have triplets during her breeding life?

Trial outcome: *This means that this ewe* ***did not have triplets*** *during her breeding life.*

ISBN: 9780170415996

Fully describe a single trial for the following situations.

1 Somebody who knows nothing about the topic guesses multi-choice answers in a 14-question test, where there are six possibilities for each question, only one of which is correct.

You are interested in how many questions they are likely to answer correctly, and the probability that this person will get five or more correct answers.

Dice results are as shown in the table:

Outcome	Correct answer	Incorrect answer
Probability	$\frac{1}{6}$	$\frac{5}{6}$
Number on die	1	2, 3, 4, 5, 6

One trial consists of ______________________________

____

I will do ________ **trials.**

Example of one trial:

Number	6	3	3	5	1	1	1	5	2	2	6	4	2	1
Outcome														

a How many correct answers were there in this trial?

Trial outcome: This means that ______________________________

____

____

____

____

b Were there five or more correct answers in this trial?

Trial outcome: This means that ______________________________

____

____

____

____

 ISBN: 9780170415996

2 The farmer also has a flock of nine nanny goats and estimates the following probabilities:

Probability (nanny goat produces a single kid) = 0.2
Probability (nanny goat produces twins) = 0.5
Probability (nanny goat produces triplets) = 0.3

You are interested in how many kids the flock is likely to produce, and the probability that the flock produces at least 20 kids.

Random numbers are used as shown in the table:

Number of kids	1	2	3
Probability	0.2	0.5	0.3
Random number	1 to 2	3 to 7	8 to 10

One trial consists of ______________________________

____

I will do ________ **trials.**

Example of one trial:

Random number	5	7	1	9	6	5	1	2	1
Number of kids									

a How many kids were produced in this trial?

Trial outcome: This means that ______________________________

____

____

____

____

b Did the flock produce at least 20 kids in this trial?

Trial outcome: This means that ______________________________

____

____

____

____

ISBN: 9780170415996

3 Nick's grandmother says that she will pay Nick $5 for every Achieved grade he gets in Mathematics, $10 for every Merit grade and $20 for every Excellence grade. He will be attempting five standards and he does not think he will fail any. At the start of the year, he estimates the following probabilities for his grades:

Probability (Achieved) = 0.5 Probability (Merit) = $\frac{1}{3}$ Probability (Excellence) = $\frac{1}{6}$

He is interested in how much his grandmother is likely to pay him, and the probability that she pays him at least $50.

The numbers on the die are used as shown in the table:

Grade	A	M	E
Probability	0.5	$\frac{1}{3}$	$\frac{1}{6}$
Numbers	1, 2, 3	4, 5	6

One trial consists of ______________________________

____

I will do ________ **trials.**

Example of one trial:

Random number	1	4	2	1	5
Grade					
Money earned ($)					

a How much would his grandmother have paid him in this trial?

Trial outcome: This means that ______________________________

____

____

____

____

b In this trial, would she have paid him at least $50?

Trial outcome: This means that ______________________________

____

____

____

____

ISBN: 9780170415996

4 The library restricts the number of books that can be borrowed to six. They found, for their customers who borrowed books, the following probabilities for the numbers of books borrowed:

Probability (person takes out 1 book) = 0.1
Probability (person takes out 2 books) = 0.35
Probability (person takes out 3 books) = 0.25
Probability (person takes out 4 books) = 0.15
Probability (person takes out 5 books) = 0.1
Probability (person takes out 6 books) = 0.05

You are interested in the number of books in total taken out by the first 10 customers of the day, and the probability that these customers take out fewer than 30 books in total.

Random numbers are used as shown in the table:

Number of books	1	2	3	4	5	6
Probability	0.1	0.35	0.25	0.15	0.1	0.05
Random number	1 to 10	11 to 45	46 to 70	71 to 85	86 to 95	96 to 100

One trial consists of ____

____

I will do ________ **trials.**

Example of one trial:

Random number	83	73	88	13	47	3	20	86	62	57
Number of books										

Trial outcomes:

____

____

____

____

____

____

____

3 Create a table, calculate your results and write them in a sentence

You must create a table that includes the following information:

- Trial number.
- Output from your device (playing card, random numbers, etc.).
- Outcome from each random number.
- Outcomes from each trial. Example: How long a ewe is allowed to breed.
- The totals required for your calculations.

Example 1: A soft drink promotion involves collecting bottle caps which have one of the following letters printed on the inside: S, N, A, P. Amy bought a bottle each day from the school canteen. The soft drink company has distributed caps with the following probabilities for each letter:

Letter	S	N	A	P
Probability	0.4	0.3	0.2	0.1
Playing card	Ace (1), 2, 3, 4	5, 6, 7	8, 9	10

One trial consists of *drawing cards from the pack, with replacement,* ***until*** *at least one of each letter has been produced.*

I have ***coloured*** *the numbers for the first time each letter occurs.*

Columns for trial outcomes.

Trial number	Results from cards or random numbers	Total needed to complete 'SNAP'	'SNAP' in ≤ 12
1	**1** 4 **8** 1 2 1 9 3 3 2 9 8 2 8 **5** 4 8 **10** **S** S **A** S S S A S S S A A S A **N** S A **P**	18	✗
2	**7** **8** **2** 9 4 2 2 1 5 8 8 9 7 1 2 5 1 8 **10** **N** **A** **S** A S S S S N A A A N S S N S A P	19	✗
3	**4** 2 **8** 8 2 4 2 9 8 1 8 **7** 3 9 3 6 **10** **S** S **A** A S S S A A S A **N** S A S N **P**	17	✗
4	**6** **1** 1 **10** 6 6 4 1 10 2 **9** **N** **S** S **P** N N S S P S **A**	11	✓
5	**9** 8 9 8 **6** **2** **10** **A** A A A **N** **S** **P**	7	✓
6	**9** **5** 5 8 8 8 6 6 **2** 3 5 6 4 2 1 **10** **A** **N** N A A A N N **S** S N N S S S **P**	16	✗
7	**1** **9** 2 2 8 **7** 1 9 9 7 7 5 **10** **S** **A** S S A **N** S A A N N N **P**	13	✗
8	**8** 8 **6** 9 **1** 5 8 1 7 2 9 2 9 3 5 3 4 2 4 7 2 8 3 **10** **A** A **N** A **S** N A S N S A S A S N S S S S N S A S **P**	24	✗
9	**6** **1** 6 5 **10** 2 2 6 2 10 4 **9** **N** **S** N N **P** S S N S P S **A**	12	✓

ISBN: 9780170415996

10	2 4 3 8 7 1 10 S S S A N S P	7	✓
11	7 7 10 10 3 6 4 6 4 4 8 N N P P S N S N S S A	11	✓
12	7 8 7 3 3 9 6 3 10 N A N S S A N S P	9	✓
13	4 6 1 6 10 5 4 10 10 1 7 1 8 S N S N P N S P P S N S A	13	✗
14	2 4 7 5 2 1 7 10 4 7 7 6 6 5 10 7 10 5 6 10 5 7 5 2 8 S S N N S S N P S N N N N N P N P N N P N N N S A	25	✗
15	3 7 1 6 10 7 7 3 4 9 S N S N P N N S S A	10	✓
16	8 1 2 3 8 7 9 6 7 9 2 8 8 9 10 A S S S A N A N N A S A A A P	15	✗
17	2 6 2 9 8 1 3 7 6 6 4 9 1 2 3 7 4 5 7 2 7 4 6 2 10 S N S A A S S N N N S A S S S N S N N S N S N S P	25	✗
18	7 9 1 9 5 2 7 4 4 8 2 6 4 9 1 10 N A S A N S N S S A S N S A S P	16	✗
19	8 9 1 7 1 8 4 3 10 A A S N S A S S P	9	✓
20	3 4 1 8 10 9 6 S S S A P A N	7	✓
	Totals:	**284**	**9**

a Estimate the number of bottle caps Amy needs in order to complete the word 'SNAP'.

Expected number of caps Amy needs to complete the work 'SNAP'

$$= \frac{\text{Total number of caps for 20 trials}}{\text{Number of trials}} = \frac{284}{20}$$

$= 14.2$

b Estimate the probability that she completes the word 'SNAP' from 12 caps or fewer.

Probability that she completes the word 'SNAP' with 12 caps or fewer

$$= \frac{\text{Number of trials with 'SNAP' from 12 caps or fewer}}{\text{Number of trials}} = \frac{9}{20}$$

$= 0.45$

Compare these results with your estimates on page 16.

Example 2: A farmer has a small flock of sheep and, from his lambing records, knows the following probabilities:

Probability (sheep produces a single lamb) = 0.49
Probability (sheep produces twins) = 0.45
Probability (sheep produces triplets) = 0.06

The farmer retires his ewes from breeding after a ewe produces single lambs for two years in a row, or after six years of breeding, whichever comes first.

Number of lambs	1	2	3
Probability	0.49	0.45	0.06
Random number	1 to 49	50 to 94	95 to 100

One trial consists of *finding random numbers from 1 to 100* ***until*** *two of the numbers 1 to 49 are produced consecutively, or six numbers are found.*

I have coloured the last year in which a ewe was allowed to breed.

Trial number	Random numbers and numbers of lambs						Number of years	Triplets
1	56	71	13	92	66	57	6	✗
	2	2	1	2	2	**2**		
2	82	25	49				3	✗
	2	1	**1**					
3	9	57	5	11			4	✓
	1	2	1	**1**				
4	17	48					2	✗
	1	**1**						
5	89	37	24				3	✗
	2	1	**1**					
6	91	2	68	77	56	94	6	✗
	2	1	2	2	2	**2**		
7	100	64	25	78	59	7	6	✓
	3	2	1	2	2	**1**		
8	93	50	43	21			4	✗
	2	2	1	**1**				
9	61	18	50	23	83	53	6	✗
	2	1	2	1	2	**2**		
10	21	28					2	✗
	1	**1**						

ISBN: 9780170415996

11	85	56	15	90	28	51	6	✗
	2	2	1	2	1	**2**		
12	20	34					2	✗
	1	**1**						
13	59	16	5				3	✓
	2	1	**1**					
14	86	64	46	21			4	✗
	2	2	1	**1**				
15	89	2	73	16	50	47	6	✗
	2	1	2	1	2	**1**		
16	4	4					2	✗
	1	**1**						
17	30	16					2	✗
	1	**1**						
18	20	55	71	11	11		5	✗
	1	2	2	1	**1**			
19	96	96	64	97	32	95	6	✓
	3	3	2	3	1	**3**		
20	97	32	14				3	✓
	3	1	**1**					
						Totals:	**81**	**5**

a Estimate the mean number of years that he allows each ewe to breed.

Mean number of years each ewe is allowed to breed

$= \frac{\text{Total number of years for 20 trials}}{\text{Number of trials}} = \frac{81}{20}$

$= 4.05$

b Estimate the probability that a ewe breeds for six years.

Probability that a ewe breeds for six years

$= \frac{\text{Number of trials where ewe bred for six years}}{\text{Number of trials}} = \frac{7}{20}$

$= 0.35$

c Estimate the probability that a ewe has triplets during her breeding life.

Probability that a ewe has triplets

$= \frac{\text{Number of trials where ewe had triplets}}{\text{Number of trials}} = \frac{5}{20}$

$= 0.25$

Compare these results with your estimates on page 16.

Complete the following tables and calculations.

1 Somebody who knows nothing about the topic guesses multi-choice answers in a 14-question test, where there are six possibilities for each question, only one of which is correct.

You are interested in how many questions they are likely to answer correctly, and the probability that this person will get five or more correct answers.

Outcome	Correct answer	Incorrect answer
Probability	$\frac{1}{6}$	$\frac{5}{6}$
Number on die	1	2, 3, 4, 5, 6

There are three 1s, so there are three correct answers.

Trial number	Results from dice or random numbers	Number of correct answers	Five or more correct?
1	2 2 2 3 1 1 4 5 5 2 4 4 1 4	3	✗
2	5 4 5 2 3 3 1 3 4 6 6 2 1 2		
3	1 5 4 6 5 2 2 6 3 6 4 3 5 4		
4	6 1 5 1 1 5 1 3 1 1 3 2 3 5		
5	5 6 5 5 3 3 3 1 6 3 3 6 4 3		
6	5 6 4 3 3 4 6 2 6 1 3 5 3 6		
7	2 2 4 2 3 2 4 2 1 3 1 2 4 4		
8	2 2 5 2 2 3 6 1 5 6 5 4 3 6		
9	1 4 2 2 5 2 5 5 4 6 2 2 4 2		
10	3 6 1 2 1 1 5 5 5 5 6 1 3 2		
11	5 6 6 5 3 1 3 5 4 2 3 1 5 6		
12	1 5 6 2 3 2 1 2 3 1 6 3 6 3		
13	6 5 6 4 4 6 3 1 2 2 6 6 2 3		
14	4 1 5 3 2 5 4 2 2 2 6 5 4 3		

ISBN: 9780170415996

Trial number	Results from dice or random numbers	Number of correct answers	Five or more correct?
15	6 5 2 4 1 5 6 3 6 4 2 1 1 5		
16	6 2 4 2 6 6 4 1 6 4 5 1 4 4		
17	6 4 2 1 6 1 3 1 3 3 2 3 6 4		
18	6 2 4 5 2 1 1 1 1 5 4 3 3 5		
19	4 4 1 3 2 3 6 1 1 1 1 5 5 1		
20	6 1 3 4 4 4 3 1 4 1 2 2 5 1		
21	3 4 5 4 1 1 1 6 4 2 5 4 5 4		
22	2 5 1 3 1 3 4 5 4 2 6 4 1 5		
23	2 4 5 6 5 6 2 4 5 1 3 2 3 6		
24	5 1 6 3 5 2 3 2 4 6 2 2 4 2		
25	2 5 6 3 6 4 3 1 6 2 4 5 2 6		
	Totals:	**60**	**2**

a Estimate the mean number of correct answers.

Mean number of correct answers

$$= \frac{\text{Total number of correct answers in 25 trials}}{\text{Number of trials}} = \frac{60}{}$$

$$= \underline{}$$

b Estimate the probability of getting five or more correct answers.

Probability of five or more correct answers

$$= \frac{}{\text{Number of trials}} = \frac{}{25}$$

$$= \underline{}$$

2 The farmer also has a flock of nine nanny goats and estimates the following probabilities:

Probability (nanny goat produces a single kid) = 0.2
Probability (nanny goat produces twins) = 0.5
Probability (nanny goat produces triplets) = 0.3

You are interested in how many kids the flock is likely to produce, and the probability that the flock produces at least 20 kids.

Number of kids	1	2	3
Probability	0.2	0.5	0.3
Random number	1 to 2	3 to 7	8 to 10

Trial number	**Random numbers and numbers of kids**									**Total number of kids**	**≥ 20?**
1	8	6	9	2	8	10	5	6	8	22	✓
	3	2	3	1							
2	6	6	3	8	5	1	5	2	1		
3	4	7	1	9	3	8	3	1	10		
4	8	10	1	7	4	4	6	8	4		
5	1	6	2	9	9	10	4	8	5		
6	6	9	7	7	5	7	4	8	5		
7	9	9	2	2	5	6	5	6	5		
8	10	10	5	10	7	9	9	1	5		
9	4	3	8	1	6	4	2	7	5		
10	4	10	10	7	7	4	5	10	6		

ISBN: 9780170415996

11	4	1	9	5	4	1	3	6	8		
12	1	2	2	3	6	6	1	9	3		
13	2	5	3	4	10	3	1	9	4		
14	6	3	5	1	6	6	3	3	6		
15	5	7	6	9	3	6	3	1	10		
16	6	8	6	3	1	6	3	5	9		
17	8	1	3	3	7	8	9	1	5		
18	2	1	3	6	4	6	5	2	2		
19	1	1	10	6	1	4	6	3	8		
20	2	2	9	8	1	9	3	10	6		
									Totals:		

a Estimate the mean number of kids produced.

Mean number of kids produced =

=

= ____________

b Estimate the probability that the flock produces 20 kids or more.

____

____

____

ISBN: 9780170415996

3 Nick's grandmother says that she will pay Nick $5 for every Achieved grade he gets in Mathematics, $10 for every Merit grade and $20 for every Excellence grade. He will be attempting five standards and he does not think he will fail any. At the start of the year, he estimates the following probabilities for his grades:

Probability (Achieved) = 0.5 Probability (Merit) = $\frac{1}{3}$ Probability (Excellence) = $\frac{1}{6}$

He is interested in how much his grandmother is likely to pay him, and the probability that she pays him at least $50.

Grade	A	M	E
Probability	0.5	$\frac{1}{3}$	$\frac{1}{6}$
Numbers	1, 2, 3	4, 5	6

Trial number	**Number on die, grades and money earned**					**Total money earned ($)**	**At least $50?**
	1	3	2	1	1		
1	A						
	$5						
	3	5	3	5	5		
2							
	2	4	2	6	2		
3							
	6	1	6	1	6		
4							
	3	6	1	6	2		
5							

ISBN: 9780170415996

<table>
<tr><td rowspan="3">6</td><td>5</td><td>5</td><td>2</td><td>2</td><td>6</td><td rowspan="3"></td><td rowspan="3"></td></tr>
<tr><td></td><td></td><td></td><td></td><td></td></tr>
<tr><td></td><td></td><td></td><td></td><td></td></tr>
<tr><td rowspan="3">7</td><td>5</td><td>4</td><td>2</td><td>5</td><td>2</td><td rowspan="3"></td><td rowspan="3"></td></tr>
<tr><td></td><td></td><td></td><td></td><td></td></tr>
<tr><td></td><td></td><td></td><td></td><td></td></tr>
<tr><td rowspan="3">8</td><td>4</td><td>3</td><td>4</td><td>5</td><td>6</td><td rowspan="3"></td><td rowspan="3"></td></tr>
<tr><td></td><td></td><td></td><td></td><td></td></tr>
<tr><td></td><td></td><td></td><td></td><td></td></tr>
<tr><td rowspan="3">9</td><td>3</td><td>2</td><td>2</td><td>1</td><td>4</td><td rowspan="3"></td><td rowspan="3"></td></tr>
<tr><td></td><td></td><td></td><td></td><td></td></tr>
<tr><td></td><td></td><td></td><td></td><td></td></tr>
<tr><td rowspan="3">10</td><td>5</td><td>6</td><td>5</td><td>1</td><td>5</td><td rowspan="3"></td><td rowspan="3"></td></tr>
<tr><td></td><td></td><td></td><td></td><td></td></tr>
<tr><td></td><td></td><td></td><td></td><td></td></tr>
<tr><td rowspan="3">11</td><td>1</td><td>1</td><td>1</td><td>3</td><td>2</td><td rowspan="3"></td><td rowspan="3"></td></tr>
<tr><td></td><td></td><td></td><td></td><td></td></tr>
<tr><td></td><td></td><td></td><td></td><td></td></tr>
<tr><td rowspan="3">12</td><td>3</td><td>3</td><td>1</td><td>5</td><td>3</td><td rowspan="3"></td><td rowspan="3"></td></tr>
<tr><td></td><td></td><td></td><td></td><td></td></tr>
<tr><td></td><td></td><td></td><td></td><td></td></tr>
<tr><td rowspan="3">13</td><td>6</td><td>2</td><td>2</td><td>4</td><td>4</td><td rowspan="3"></td><td rowspan="3"></td></tr>
<tr><td></td><td></td><td></td><td></td><td></td></tr>
<tr><td></td><td></td><td></td><td></td><td></td></tr>
</table>

14	6	5	4	1	4		
15	5	1	3	1	2		
16	3	1	4	3	3		
17	3	6	4	4	1		
18	6	2	6	5	2		
					Totals:		

a Estimate how much his grandmother will pay him.

b Estimate the probability that she pays him at least $50.

 ISBN: 9780170415996

4 The library restricts the number of books that can be borrowed to six. They found, for their customers who borrowed books, the following probabilities for the numbers of books borrowed:

Probability (person takes out 1 book) = 0.1
Probability (person takes out 2 books) = 0.35
Probability (person takes out 3 books) = 0.25
Probability (person takes out 4 books) = 0.15
Probability (person takes out 5 books) = 0.1
Probability (person takes out 6 books) = 0.05

You are interested in the number of books in total taken out by the first 10 customers of the day, and the probability that these customers take out fewer than 30 books in total.

Number of books	1	2	3	4	5	6
Probability	0.1	0.35	0.25	0.15	0.1	0.05
Random number	1 to 10	11 to 45	46 to 70	71 to 85	86 to 95	96 to 100

To save time, most of this table has been completed for you.

Trial number	**Random numbers and numbers of books**										**Total number of books**	**< 30?**
1	23	91	83	41	46	96	86	49	43	63		
2	35	68	94	42	4	6	68	90	16	43		
3	27	4	30	72	28	16	67	18	63	88	26	
	2	1	2	4	2	2	3	2	3	5		
4	29	6	51	27	14	27	2	77	98	81	27	
	2	1	3	2	2	2	1	4	6	4		
5	70	51	60	62	21	2	42	87	34	16	26	
	3	3	3	3	2	1	2	5	2	2		
6	12	45	50	69	21	91	79	39	16	61	28	
	2	2	3	3	2	5	4	2	2	3		

ISBN: 9780170415996

Trial number	Random numbers and numbers of books										Total number of books	< 30?
7	96	95	79	11	16	6	5	83	57	41	30	
	6	5	4	2	2	1	1	4	3	2		
8	50	54	100	40	73	49	28	46	70	49	32	
	3	3	6	2	4	3	2	3	3	3		
9	8	36	92	80	64	57	21	31	25	71	28	
	1	2	5	4	3	3	2	2	2	4		
10	50	27	51	87	14	69	96	63	97	73	37	
	3	2	3	5	2	3	6	3	6	4		
11	63	54	69	13	21	89	81	5	31	58	28	
	3	3	3	2	2	5	4	1	2	3		
12	72	34	55	78	11	60	95	43	30	11	29	
	4	2	3	4	2	3	5	2	2	2		
13	32	7	76	93	18	69	100	34	26	88	32	
	2	1	4	5	2	3	6	2	2	5		
14	57	45	38	44	30	73	24	77	63	56	27	
	3	2	2	2	2	4	2	4	3	3		
15	9	86	30	83	5	84	29	6	27	96	28	
	1	5	2	4	1	4	2	1	2	6		
16	3	49	58	6	67	95	99	64	9	97	32	
	1	3	3	1	3	5	6	3	1	6		
17	60	58	33	98	38	12	11	99	21	54	31	
	3	3	2	6	2	2	2	6	2	3		

ISBN: 9780170415996

<table>
<tr><td rowspan="2">18</td><td>93</td><td>3</td><td>78</td><td>20</td><td>92</td><td>99</td><td>26</td><td>42</td><td>56</td><td>38</td><td rowspan="2">32</td><td rowspan="2"></td></tr>
<tr><td>5</td><td>1</td><td>4</td><td>2</td><td>5</td><td>6</td><td>2</td><td>2</td><td>3</td><td>2</td></tr>
<tr><td rowspan="2">19</td><td>33</td><td>67</td><td>61</td><td>66</td><td>59</td><td>32</td><td>22</td><td>78</td><td>96</td><td>47</td><td rowspan="2">31</td><td rowspan="2"></td></tr>
<tr><td>2</td><td>3</td><td>3</td><td>3</td><td>3</td><td>2</td><td>2</td><td>4</td><td>6</td><td>3</td></tr>
<tr><td rowspan="2">20</td><td>73</td><td>38</td><td>7</td><td>22</td><td>3</td><td>42</td><td>21</td><td>78</td><td>94</td><td>80</td><td rowspan="2">27</td><td rowspan="2"></td></tr>
<tr><td>4</td><td>2</td><td>1</td><td>2</td><td>1</td><td>2</td><td>2</td><td>4</td><td>5</td><td>4</td></tr>
<tr><td rowspan="2">21</td><td>63</td><td>36</td><td>87</td><td>96</td><td>10</td><td>31</td><td>49</td><td>34</td><td>99</td><td>34</td><td rowspan="2">32</td><td rowspan="2"></td></tr>
<tr><td>3</td><td>2</td><td>5</td><td>6</td><td>1</td><td>2</td><td>3</td><td>2</td><td>6</td><td>2</td></tr>
<tr><td rowspan="2">22</td><td>62</td><td>34</td><td>96</td><td>95</td><td>64</td><td>38</td><td>100</td><td>14</td><td>10</td><td>46</td><td rowspan="2">33</td><td rowspan="2"></td></tr>
<tr><td>3</td><td>2</td><td>6</td><td>5</td><td>3</td><td>2</td><td>6</td><td>2</td><td>1</td><td>3</td></tr>
<tr><td rowspan="2">23</td><td>90</td><td>55</td><td>98</td><td>14</td><td>7</td><td>26</td><td>84</td><td>77</td><td>25</td><td>7</td><td rowspan="2">30</td><td rowspan="2"></td></tr>
<tr><td>5</td><td>3</td><td>6</td><td>2</td><td>1</td><td>2</td><td>4</td><td>4</td><td>2</td><td>1</td></tr>
<tr><td rowspan="2">24</td><td>38</td><td>2</td><td>63</td><td>75</td><td>78</td><td>49</td><td>21</td><td>13</td><td>84</td><td>28</td><td rowspan="2">27</td><td rowspan="2"></td></tr>
<tr><td>2</td><td>1</td><td>3</td><td>4</td><td>4</td><td>3</td><td>2</td><td>2</td><td>4</td><td>2</td></tr>
<tr><td rowspan="2">25</td><td>56</td><td>39</td><td>91</td><td>5</td><td>57</td><td>55</td><td>72</td><td>68</td><td>35</td><td>81</td><td rowspan="2">30</td><td rowspan="2"></td></tr>
<tr><td>3</td><td>2</td><td>5</td><td>1</td><td>3</td><td>3</td><td>4</td><td>3</td><td>2</td><td>4</td></tr>
<tr><td colspan="11">Totals:</td><td></td><td></td></tr>
</table>

a Estimate the mean number of books taken out by the first 10 borrowers in the day.

b Estimate the probability the first 10 borrowers of the day took out fewer than 30 books in total.

ISBN: 9780170415996

4 Discussion and assumptions

Make it clear that you understand that:

- your simulation results are only **estimates** of the true values of means and probabilities
- if you had done **more trials**, you would have been able to make **more reliable estimates**
- if you repeated your simulation, you would almost certainly get **different results**.

Assumptions:

- Your chosen device produces numbers that are truly **random**.
  For instance, the die is a fair die, and not loaded to produce more of any one number.

- That events are **independent**. This means that the outcome from one event does not affect the outcome from any other event.
  For instance, getting a bottle cap with an 'S' does not have any effect on which letter is under the next cap.

- The probabilities of each outcome remain **constant** throughout the simulation.
  For instance, the probability that a ewe has triplets does not change as the ewe gets older.

You need to link:

Assumption ⇒ simulation process ⇒ effect on results

Example:

Assumption

It is assumed that the probability that a ewe will have a single lamb remains constant throughout the simulation. However, if a ewe has a single lamb in one year, she may be more likely to have single lambs in following years.

Simulation process

However, in the simulation, the probability of having single lambs remains constant, so for ewes that have already had single lambs, this simulation probability may be too low.

Effect on results

Therefore the estimate for the mean number of years a ewe is allowed to breed would be higher than the true mean.

ISBN: 9780170415996

Example 1: A soft drink promotion involves collecting bottle caps which have one of the following letters printed on the inside: S, N, A, P. Amy bought a bottle each day from the school canteen. The soft drink company has distributed caps with the following probabilities for each letter:

Letter	S	N	A	P
Probability	0.4	0.3	0.2	0.1

From the simulation with 30 trials:

a *The mean number of caps Amy requires in order to complete the word 'SNAP' = 12.43.*

b *The probability that she completes the word 'SNAP' from 12 caps = 0.6.*

- *Both of these values are only estimates of their true values.*
- *If I had done more than 30 trials, my estimates would probably have been more reliable.*
- *If I repeated the simulation, I would almost certainly get different results.*

I assumed that, for bottles sold at the canteen, the probabilities of getting each letter were similar to those for all the bottles distributed by the company. If that was not the case and, say, the canteen stocked mostly bottles with an 'S' under the cap, then the probabilities used in the simulation would not reflect the actual situation. If most of the bottles had an 'S' under the cap, then the estimated mean number of caps needed to complete the word 'SNAP' would be higher and the estimated probability of completing the word 'SNAP' from 12 caps would be lower.

I assumed that Amy did not swap caps with anybody else. If she had, then it would probably have been much easier for her to complete the word 'SNAP'. I used my original simulation results and assumed that:

- *as soon as Amy got a second of either of the rarest letters (A or P), she swapped it for whichever of those two (A or P) that she needed.*
- *she did just one swap.*

In the table I have ***highlighted*** *the first spare of either of these letters (random numbers 8, 9 or 10), and recalculated the number of caps needed to complete the word. I have also recorded whether she completed the word with 12 caps or fewer.*

Trial number	Results from cards or random numbers	Total needed to complete 'SNAP'	'SNAP' in ≤12
1	1 4 8 1 2 1 **9** 3 3 2 9 8 2 8 5 4 8 10	15	✗
2	7 8 2 7 4 2 2 1 5 **8** 8 9 7 1 2 5 1 8 10	10	✓
3	4 2 8 8 2 4 2 9 8 1 8 7 3 **9** 3 6 10	14	✗
4	6 1 1 10 6 6 4 1 **10** 2 9	9	✓
5	9 **8** 9 8 6 2 10	6	✓
6	9 5 5 **8** 8 8 6 6 2 3 5 6 4 2 1 10	9	✓

ISBN: 9780170415996

7	1 9 2 2 8 7 1 9 9 7 7 5 10	6	✓
8	8 8 6 9 1 5 8 1 7 2 9 2 9 3 5 3 4 2 4 7 2 8 3 10	5	✓
9	6 1 6 5 10 2 2 6 2 10 4 9	10	✓
10	2 4 3 8 7 1 10	7	✓
11	7 7 10 10 3 6 4 6 4 4 8	5	✓
12	7 8 7 3 3 9 6 3 10	6	✓
13	4 6 1 6 10 5 4 10 10 1 7 1 8	8	✓
14	2 4 7 5 2 1 7 10 4 7 7 6 6 5 10 7 10 5 6 10 5 7 5 2 8	15	✗
15	3 7 1 6 10 7 7 3 4 9	10	✓
16	8 1 2 3 8 7 9 6 7 9 2 8 8 9 10	6	✓
17	2 6 2 9 8 1 3 7 6 6 4 9 1 2 3 7 4 5 7 2 7 4 6 2 10	5	✓
18	7 9 1 9 5 2 7 4 4 8 2 6 4 9 1 10	4	✓
19	8 9 1 7 1 8 4 3 10	6	✓
20	3 4 1 8 10 9 6	6	✓
	Totals:	**162**	**17**

a *Estimate the number of bottle caps Amy needs in order to complete the word 'SNAP'.*

Expected number of caps Amy needs to complete the word 'SNAP'

$$= \frac{\text{Total number of caps for 20 trials}}{\text{Number of trials}} = \frac{162}{20} = 8.1$$

b *Estimate the probability that she completes the word SNAP from 12 caps or fewer.*

Probability that she complete the word 'SNAP' with 12 caps or fewer

$$= \frac{\text{Number of trials with 'SNAP' from 12 caps or fewer}}{\text{Number of trials}} = \frac{17}{20} = 0.85$$

If she did just one swap of caps, it reduced the mean number of caps needed to complete the word 'SNAP' from 14.2 to 8.1. It also increased the probability of completing the word with 12 caps or fewer from 0.45 to 0.85. There were only two trials (numbers 10 and 15) in which swapping made no difference.

 ISBN: 9780170415996

Example 2: A farmer has a small flock of sheep and, from his lambing records, knows the following probabilities:

Probability (ewe produces a single lamb) = 0.49
Probability (ewe produces twins) = 0.45
Probability (ewe produces triplets) = 0.06

The farmer retires his ewes from breeding after a ewe produces single lambs for two years in a row, or after **six** years of breeding, whichever comes first.

From the simulation with 20 trials:

a *The mean number of years that he allows each ewe to breed = 4.05*
b *The probability that a ewe breeds for six years = 0.35*
c *The probability that a ewe has triplets during her breeding life = 0.25*

- *This mean and the probabilities are only estimates of their true values.*
- *If I had done more than 20 trials, my estimates would probably have been more reliable.*
- *If I repeated the simulation, I would almost certainly get different results.*

It is assumed that the probability that a ewe will have a single lamb remains constant throughout the simulation. However, if a ewe has a single lamb in one year, she may be more likely to have single lambs in following years. However, in the simulation, the probability of having single lambs remains constant, so for ewes that have already had single lambs, this simulation probability may be too low. Therefore the estimate for the mean number of years a ewe is allowed to breed would be higher than the true mean.

I have assumed that the probabilities for his ewes having single lambs, twins or triplets are based on data from his own ewes from previous years. However, these probabilities may not be very reliable for several reasons:

1 *He has a small flock, so it is unlikely that probabilities calculated from a small sample are reliable.*

2 *He is preventing ewes that have single lambs for two years in a row from breeding again. I think that this means that the probabilities for having twins and triplets is likely to increase over the years, and that for single lambs will decrease. If, in the simulation, the probabilities of having twins or triplets are lower than in reality, then the estimated mean and two probabilities calculated will also be lower than the actual values.*

3 *The probabilities may vary depending on the rams that mated with the ewes. If he used different rams each year, the probabilities of having single lambs, twins and triplets may change.*

Write discussions and assumptions for each of the following.

1 Somebody who knows nothing about the topic guesses multi-choice answers in a 14-question test, where there are six possibilities for each question, only one of which is correct. You are interested in how many questions they answer correctly.

Mean number of correct answers = 2.55

Probability of getting five or more correct answers = 0.08

ISBN: 9780170415996

2 The farmer also has a flock of nine nanny goats and estimates the following probabilities:

Probability (nanny goat produces a single kid) = 0.2
Probability (nanny goat produces twins) = 0.5
Probability (nanny goat produces triplets) = 0.3

You are interested in how many kids the flock produces.

Mean number of kids = 18.5

Probability that the flock produced 20 kids or more = 0.3

ISBN: 9780170415996

3 Nick's grandmother says that she will pay Nick \$5 for every Achieved grade he gets in Mathematics, \$10 for every Merit grade and \$20 for every Excellence grade. He will be attempting five standards and he does not think he will fail any. At the start of the year, he estimates the following probabilities for his grades:

Probability (Achieved) = 0.5 Probability (Merit) = $\frac{1}{3}$ Probability (Excellence) = $\frac{1}{6}$

Estimate of how much his grandmother will pay him = \$44.17

Probability that she pays him at least \$50 = 0.5

ISBN: 9780170415996

4 The library restricts the number of books that can be borrowed to six. They found, for their customers who borrowed, the following probabilities for the numbers of books borrowed:

Probability (person takes out 1 book) = 0.1
Probability (person takes out 2 books) = 0.35
Probability (person takes out 3 books) = 0.25
Probability (person takes out 4 books) = 0.15
Probability (person takes out 5 books) = 0.1
Probability (person takes out 6 books) = 0.05

Mean number of books taken out by the first 10 borrowers in the day = 29.76

Probability the first 10 borrowers of the day took out fewer than 30 books in total = 0.48

Putting it all together

1 State which device you will use and describe how you will use it

Step 1: Make sure that you:
- know what all the possible outcomes are
- know the probability of each outcome
- check that all these probabilities add to 1.

Step 2: The device I will use is: ______________________

Step 3: This is how I will use my device: ______________________

____

____

Step 4: Create a table showing:

Every possible outcome				
Probability of each outcome				
Random numbers, numbers from dice, etc.				

Which results from your device will represent each outcome.

2 Describe one trial

One trial consists of ______________________

until ______________________

I will do ________ **trials.**

Note: You should do at least 30 trials.

Example of one trial: Complete a table including at least the following:

From your device, e.g. random number.

Include enough columns for you to be able to complete **one** trial.

Number						
Outcome						

What happens in the context of the simulation.

Trial outcome: This means that ______________________

____

 ISBN: 9780170415996

3 Create a table, calculate your results and write them in a sentence

You must create a table that includes the following information:

- Trial number.
- Output from your device (playing card, random numbers, etc.).
- Outcome from each random number.
- Outcomes from each trial. Example: How long a ewe is allowed to breed.

On every second row you usually need to list the outcomes from each random number.

Columns for trial outcomes.

Trial number	Results from cards or random numbers		
1			
2			
29			
30			
	Totals:		

My estimate of the probability of .... = *(Total number of ___ from ___ trials)* / *Number of trials*

=

My estimate of the mean number of .... = *(Total number of trials with ________)* / *Number of trials*

=

4 Discussion and assumptions

Make it clear that you understand:

- you found only **estimates** of the true values
- **more trials** means **more reliable estimates**
- repeating the simulation would give **different results**.

Remember, you need to link: **Assumption ⇒ simulation process ⇒ effect on results**

ISBN: 9780170415996

Practice simulation

The beetle game

Geeti is playing a game with her little brother.

- Each of them aims to be the first to complete their model of a beetle.
- They take it in turns to throw a die.
- The number on the die determines which portion of the beetle they get.

They need to allocate the numbers on the die to produce the following probabilities:

Beetle part	Head	Thorax	Wings	Feelers	Legs
Number needed	1	1	2	2	6
Probability	$\frac{1}{6}$	$\frac{1}{6}$	$\frac{1}{6}$	$\frac{1}{6}$	$\frac{1}{3}$

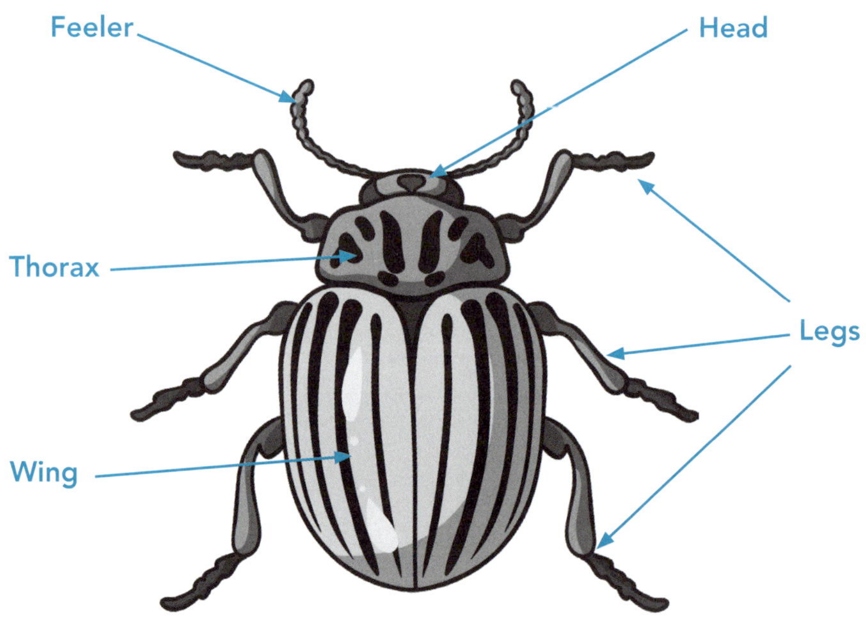

This activity requires you to design and run a simulation that can be used to investigate the number of turns it will take to complete one beetle and whether Geeti is likely to complete a beetle in 20 turns or fewer.

You are required to write a report that describes your simulation method and records its outcomes. Your report will include a conclusion based on the outcomes of your simulation, and a reflection on your process.

ISBN: 9780170415996

1 State which device you will use and describe how you will use it.

Step 1: ________ + ________ + ________ + ________ + ________ + ________ = ________

Step 2: *The device I will use is* ______________________

Step 3: *This is how I will use my device:* ______________________

____

____

____

____

Step 4:

Every possible outcome	Head	Thorax	Wings	Feelers	Legs
Probability of each outcome	$\frac{1}{6}$	$\frac{1}{6}$	$\frac{1}{6}$	$\frac{1}{6}$	$\frac{1}{3}$
Numbers on device	1	2	3	4	5 or 6

2 Describe one trial.

One trial consists of ______________________

until ______________________

____

I will do ____________ *trials.*

Example of one trial:

Number																									
Outcome																									

Trial outcome: This means that ______________________

____

____

____

____

____

ISBN: 9780170415996

3 Create a table, calculate your results and write them in a sentence.

My results:

Trial number	Results from die		
1			
2			
3			
4			
5			
6			
7			
8			
9			
10			
11			
12			
13			
14			
15			
16			
17			
18			
19			

ISBN: 9780170415996

20			
21			
22			
23			
24			
25			
26			
27			
28			
29			
30			
	Totals:		

My estimate of the mean number of ______________________

$= \dfrac{\textit{Total number of} \_\_\_\_\_\_\_\_}{\textit{Number of trials}}$

= ______

= ______

My estimate for the probability of ______________________

$= \dfrac{\textit{Number of trials with} \_\_\_\_\_\_\_\_}{\textit{Number of trials}}$

= ______

= ______

ISBN: 9780170415996

4 Discussion and assumptions:

ISBN: 9780170415996

Practice tasks

Practice task one

Papa's Pies

During June, Papa's Pies runs a promotion campaign.

- One token is given away with each pie that is sold.
- There are three types of token: one is labelled 'Pie', one is labelled 'Drink', and the third is labelled 'Movie'.
- A customer can exchange three 'Pie' tokens for a free pie, three 'Drink' tokens for a can of drink, or three 'Movie' tokens for a movie ticket.
- The table shows the percentages of each type of token released for the promotion campaign:

Token	Pie	Drink	Movie ticket
Probability	40%	40%	20%

Toby the builder buys a pie each week day for his lunch and saves up the tokens.

This activity requires you to design and run a simulation that can be used to estimate the number of pies he will need to buy in order to collect three of **any** type of token (for example: Drink, Drink, Drink), and whether it is likely or not that he will be able to claim a free movie ticket after two weeks (10 working days).

You are required to write a report that describes your simulation method and records its outcomes. Your report will include a conclusion based on the outcomes of your simulation, and a reflection on your process.

1 Device:

Step 1: ______________________________

Step 2: ______________________________

Step 3: ______________________________

____

____

Step 4:

ISBN: 9780170415996

2 **Trials:**

3 **Table, calculations and results written in a sentence:**

ISBN: 9780170415996

	Totals:		

ISBN: 9780170415996

My estimate of the mean number of ______________________

= *Total number of* ______________ / *Number of trials*

= ______

= ______

My estimate for the probability of ______________________

= *Number of trials with* ______________ / *Number of trials*

= ______

= ______

4 Discussion and assumptions:

ISBN: 9780170415996

Practice task two

Motel occupation

Guido runs a motel which has seven units, each of which sleeps a maximum of four people. From past records he estimates the following probabilities for the number of people who will occupy his motel units during March:

Number of people	0	1	2	3	4
Probability	0.06	0.22	0.45	0.09	0.18

- The daily cost of hiring a unit is $90 plus $25 per person.
- His annual average overall cost for the motel (labour, insurance, rates, maintenance, etc.) is $950 per day.

This activity requires you to design and run a simulation that can be used to investigate the total number of people who stay in his seven units during each night in March and the daily income generated by the motel. Investigate whether the motel is likely to be profitable during March.

You are required to write a report that describes your simulation method and records its outcomes. Your report will include a conclusion based on the outcomes of your simulation, and a reflection on your process.

Device:

ISBN: 9780170415996

Trials:

Table, calculations and results written in a sentence:

ISBN: 9780170415996

	Totals:		

ISBN: 9780170415996

Discussion and assumptions:

ISBN: 9780170415996

 ISBN: 9780170415996

Practice task three

Cool Cruises

Cool Cruises takes passengers on day trips. The passengers sightsee, go for bush walks and have a barbecue lunch on a beach. At the start of each trip, each passenger can select a complimentary gift. Storage space on the boat is very limited, so the cruise company is investigating the number of each gift that they take on board.

- They take 12 passengers on each cruise, and because it is so popular, each cruise is full.
- Each passenger can select from the following: a backpack, an umbrella, a bottle of sunscreen, a sun hat, or a beach towel.
- From previous cruise data, the manager knows that 21% of passengers choose a backpack, 14% choose an umbrella, 25% choose sunscreen, 8% choose a sun hat, and 32% choose a beach towel.
- Because storage space is limited, they want to carry the minimum number of each gift but still be able to give all passengers the gift they want on 90% of cruises.
- They carry 4 backpacks, 3 umbrellas, 6 bottles of sunscreen, 2 sun hats, and 6 beach towels on each cruise.

This task requires that you design and run a simulation that can be used to investigate the company's claim that all passengers will get the gift they want on 90% of cruises.

You will write a report that describes your simulation method and records its outcomes. Your report will include a conclusion based on the outcomes of your simulation, a reflection on your process, and a recommendation to the company.

ISBN: 9780170415996

ISBN: 9780170415996

  ISBN: 9780170415996

Answers

Probability revision (pp. 6–11)

Using numbers to write probabilities (p. 6)

1 $\frac{4}{13} = 0.3077$ $\frac{1}{3} = 0.\dot{3}$
Most likely: $\frac{1}{3}$

2 $\frac{3}{4} = 0.75$ $\frac{10}{13} = 0.7692$
Most likely: $\frac{10}{13}$

3 $\frac{1}{18} = 0.0\dot{5}$ $\frac{3}{57} = 0.0526$
Most likely: $\frac{1}{18}$

4 $\frac{6}{17} = 0.3529$ $\frac{4}{11} = 0.\dot{3}\dot{6}$
Most likely: $\frac{4}{11}$

5 $\frac{7}{14989}$ Highly unlikely

6 $\frac{8}{17}$ Maybe

7 $\frac{23}{32}$ Probable

8 0.9421 Very likely

9 $\frac{89}{90}$ Almost certain

10 0.0643 Slight chance

Ways of calculating probabilities (pp. 7–9)

1 Equally likely outcomes

1 $\frac{1}{6} = 0.1\dot{6}$

2 $\frac{2}{6} = \frac{1}{3} = 0.\dot{3}$

3 $\frac{3}{6} = \frac{1}{2} = 0.5$

4 $\frac{5}{6} = 0.8\dot{3}$

5 0

6 1

7 $\frac{13}{52} = \frac{1}{4} = 0.25$

8 $\frac{26}{52} = \frac{1}{2} = 0.5$

9 $\frac{4}{52} = 0.0769$

10 $\frac{2}{52} = \frac{1}{26} = 0.0385$

11 $\frac{8}{52} = \frac{2}{13} = 0.1538$

12 $\frac{8}{52} = \frac{2}{13} = 0.1538$

13 $\frac{28}{52} = \frac{7}{13} = 0.5385$

14 $\frac{44}{52} = \frac{11}{13} = 0.8462$

15 $\frac{20}{100} = \frac{1}{5} = 0.2$

16 $\frac{70}{100} = \frac{7}{10} = 0.7$

17 $\frac{50}{100} = \frac{5}{10} = 0.5$

18 $\frac{70}{100} = \frac{7}{10} = 0.7$

2 Long run relative frequency

1 a P(student came with a partner from within the school) = $\frac{96}{280} = 0.3429$

b P(student came with a partner) $= \frac{96 + 37}{280} = 0.475$

2 a P(student got an Excellence grade) $= \frac{11}{29} = 0.3793$

b P(student got neither an Excellence nor a Merit grade) = $\frac{8}{29}$ = 02759

3 a P(difference was 4) = $\frac{7}{50} = 0.14$

b P(difference was less than 3) = $\frac{33}{50} = 0.66$

4 a

	Suspect die	Fair die
P(1)	$\frac{3}{34} = 0.0882$	$\frac{1}{6} = 0.1\dot{6}$
P(1 or 2)	$\frac{6}{34}$ = 01765	$\frac{2}{6} = \frac{1}{3} = 0.\dot{3}$
P(4, 5 or 6)	$\frac{23}{34} = 0.6765$	$\frac{3}{6} = \frac{1}{2} = 0.5$
P(not a 5)	$\frac{25}{34} = 0.7353$	$\frac{5}{6} = 0.8\dot{3}$

b I would do a lot more trials than 34, say 100 or 200.

Expected number of outcomes (p. 10)

1 18 throws

2 23 or 24 picture cards

3 4 or 5 babies

4 43 or 44 students

5 19 or 20 hands

Mixing it up (p. 11)

1 0.898

2 118 or 119

3 a $\frac{7}{15} = 0.4\dot{6}$ b $\frac{11}{15} = 0.7\dot{3}$

c $\frac{4}{15} = 0.2\dot{6}$

4 0.44

5 206 or 207

6 a $\frac{13}{17} = 0.7647$ b $\frac{11}{16} = 0.6875$

 ISBN: 9780170415996

Randomness and independence (pp. 12–15)

	Independent or not independent?	Reason
1	Not independent	Being in Year 13 makes it more likely that a student is attempting Level 3 standards.
2	Independent	Studying mathematics in Year 12 is unlikely to make any difference to whether a student buys lunch from the canteen.
3	Not independent	Students in Years 11, 12 or 13 are generally more likely to skip assembly.
4	Not independent	Students are less likely to be able to afford the latest iPhone.
5	Not independent	People who plays bowls are more likely to be over 60 years old.
6	Independent	The fact that the car is grey is unlikely to affect its value.
7	Not independent	A Mercedes is more likely than other cars to be worth more than $10 000.
8	Independent	The results of previous throws will make no difference to the outcome of next throw.
9	Independent	The results of previous tosses will make no difference to the outcome of next toss.

The simulation process (pp. 17–49)

1 Using a device to simulate probabilities (pp. 17–20)

Note: Your answers may vary from those below. If they do, check them with your teacher.

1 **Step 1:** Probabilities = $\frac{1}{6} + \frac{5}{6} = 1$

Step 2: The device I will use is one die.

Step 3: This is how I will use my device:

- I will throw a six-sided die and record each number shown.
- This means that the probability of getting each of the numbers 1 to 6 is $\frac{1}{6}$.

Step 4:

Outcome	Correct answer	Incorrect answer
Probability	$\frac{1}{6}$	$\frac{5}{6}$
Number on die	1	2, 3, 4, 5, 6

2 **Step 1:** Probabilities = 0.2 + 0.5 + 0.3 = 1

Step 2: The device I will use my graphics calculator.

Step 3: This is how I will use my device:

- I will use my calculator with the formula Ran Int# (1, 10). This will produce random numbers from 1 to 10.
- I will use the numbers 1 to 10, so the probability of getting each number is 0.1.

Step 4:

Number of kids	1	2	3
Probability	0.2	0.5	0.3
Random numbers	1, 2	3, 4, 5, 6, 7	8, 9, 10

3 **Step 1:** Probabilities = $0.5 + \frac{1}{3} + \frac{1}{6} = 1$

Step 2: The device I will use my graphics calculator.

Step 3: This is how I will use my device:

- I will use my calculator with the formula Ran Int# (1, 6). This will produce random numbers from 1 to 6.
- This means that the probability of getting each of the numbers 1 to 6 is $\frac{1}{6}$.

Step 4:

Grade	A	M	E
Probability	0.5	$\frac{1}{3}$	$\frac{1}{6}$
Random numbers	1, 2, 3	4, 5	6

4 **Step 1:** Probabilities = 0.1 + 0.35 + 0.25 + 0.15 + 0.1 + 0.05 = 1

Step 2: The device I will use my graphics calculator.

Step 3: This is how I will use my device:

- I will use my calculator with the formula Ran Int# (1, 100). This will produce random numbers from 1 to 100.
- I will use the numbers 1 to 100, so the probability of getting each number is 0.01.

Step 4:

Number of books	1	2	3	4	5	6
Probability	0.1	0.35	0.25	0.15	0.1	0.05
Random numbers	1 to 10	11 to 45	46 to 70	71 to 85	86 to 95	96 to 100

ISBN: 9780170415996

2 Trials (pp. 21–27)

1 **One trial consists of** tossing a fair die 14 times.
I will do 25 **trials.**
Example of one trial:

Number	6	3	3	5	1	1	1	5	2	2	6	4	2	1
Outcome	✗	✗	✗	✗	✓	✓	✓	✗	✗	✗	✗	✗	✗	✓

a **Trial outcome:** This means that the person got four correct answers.

b **Trial outcome:** This means that the person did not get five or more questions correct.

2 **One trial consists of** finding nine random numbers between 1 and 10.
I will do 20 **trials.**
Example of one trial:

Random number	5	7	1	9	6	5	1	2	1
Number of kids	2	2	1	3	2	2	1	1	1

a **Trial outcome:** This means that his nine nanny goats produced 15 kids.

b **Trial outcome:** This means that his nine nanny goats did not produce 20 kids or more.

3 **One trial consists of** throwing the die five times and recording the numbers shown.
I will do 18 **trials.**
Example of one trial:

Random number	1	4	2	1	5
Grade	A	M	A	A	M
Money earned ($)	5	10	5	5	10

a **Trial outcome:** This means that his grandmother will pay him $35.

b **Trial outcome:** This means that in this trial she did not pay him $50.

4 **One trial consists of** finding 10 random numbers between 1 and 100.
I will do 25 **trials.**
Example of one trial:

Random number	83	73	88	13	47	3	20	86	62	57
Number of books	4	4	5	2	3	1	2	5	3	3

Trial outcomes

a This means the first 10 borrowers of the day took out a total of 32 books.

b This means that the first 10 borrowers of the day took out more than 30 books in total.

3 Create a table, calculate your results and write them in a sentence (pp. 28–41)

1

Trial number	Results from dice or random numbers	Number of correct answers	Five or more correct?
1	22231145524414	3	✗
2	51523313466212	2	✗
3	15465226364354	1	✗
4	61511513113235	6	✓
5	56553331633643	1	✗
6	56433462613536	1	✗
7	22423242131244	2	✗
8	22522361565436	1	✗
9	14225255462242	1	✗
10	36121155556132	4	✗
11	56653135423156	2	✗
12	15623212316363	3	✗
13	65644631226623	1	✗
14	41532542226543	1	✗
15	65241563642115	3	✗
16	62426641645144	2	✗
17	64216131332364	3	✗
18	62452111154335	4	✗
19	44132361111551	6	✓
20	61344431412251	4	✗
21	34541116425454	3	✗
22	25131345426415	3	✗
23	24565624513136	1	✗
24	51635232462242	1	✗
25	25636431624526	1	✗
	Totals:	60	2

a Mean number of correct answers

$$= \frac{\text{Total number of correct answers in 25 trials}}{\text{Number of trials}}$$

$$= \frac{60}{25}$$

$$= 2.4$$

b Probability of five or more correct answers

$$= \frac{\text{Number of trials resulting in five or more correct answers}}{\text{Number of trials}}$$

$$= \frac{2}{25}$$

$$= 0.08$$

 ISBN: 9780170415996

2

Trial number	Random numbers and numbers of kids	Total number of kids	≥ 20?
1	8 6 9 2 8 10 5 6 8 3 2 3 1 3 3 2 2 3	22	✓
2	6 6 3 8 5 1 5 2 1 2 2 2 3 2 1 2 1 1	16	✗
3	4 7 1 9 3 8 3 1 10 2 2 1 3 2 3 2 1 3	19	✗
4	8 10 1 7 4 4 6 8 4 3 3 1 2 2 2 2 3 2	20	✓
5	1 6 2 9 9 10 4 8 5 1 2 1 3 3 3 2 3 2	20	✓
6	6 9 7 7 5 7 4 8 5 2 3 2 2 2 2 2 3 2	20	✓
7	9 9 2 2 5 6 5 6 5 3 3 1 1 2 2 2 2 2	18	✗
8	10 10 5 10 7 9 9 1 5 3 3 2 3 2 3 3 1 2	22	✓
9	4 3 8 1 6 4 2 7 5 2 2 3 1 2 2 1 2 2	17	✗
10	4 10 10 7 7 4 5 10 6 2 3 3 2 2 2 2 3 2	21	✓
11	4 1 9 5 4 1 3 6 8 2 1 3 2 2 1 2 2 3	18	✗
12	1 2 2 3 6 6 1 9 3 1 1 1 2 2 2 1 3 2	15	✗
13	2 5 3 4 10 3 1 9 4 1 2 2 2 3 2 1 3 2	18	✗
14	6 3 5 1 6 6 3 3 6 2 2 2 1 2 2 2 2 2	17	✗
15	5 7 6 9 3 6 3 1 10 2 2 2 3 2 2 2 1 3	19	✗
16	6 8 6 3 1 6 3 5 9 2 3 2 2 1 2 2 2 3	19	✗
17	8 1 3 3 7 8 9 1 5 3 1 2 2 2 3 3 1 2	19	✗
18	2 1 3 6 4 6 5 2 2 1 1 2 2 2 2 2 1 1	14	✗
19	1 1 10 6 1 4 6 3 8 1 1 3 2 1 2 2 2 3	17	✗
20	2 2 9 8 1 9 3 10 6 1 1 3 3 1 3 2 3 2	19	✗
	Totals:	370	6

a Mean number of kids produced

$$= \frac{\text{Total number of kids in 20 trials}}{\text{Number of trials}}$$

$$= \frac{370}{20}$$

$$= 18.5$$

b Probability the flock produced 20 kids or more

$$= \frac{\text{Total number of trials in which 20 or more kids were produced}}{\text{Number of trials}}$$

$$= \frac{6}{20}$$

$$= 0.3$$

3

Trial number	Number on die, grades and money earned	Total money earned ($)	At least $50?
1	1 3 2 1 1 A A A A A 5 5 5 5 5	25	✗
2	3 5 3 5 5 A M A M M 5 10 5 10 10	40	✗
3	2 4 2 6 2 A M A E A 5 10 5 20 5	45	✗
4	6 1 6 1 6 E A E A E 20 5 20 5 20	70	✓
5	3 6 1 6 2 A E A E A 5 20 5 20 5	55	✓
6	5 5 2 2 6 M M A A E 10 10 5 5 20	50	✓
7	5 4 2 5 2 M M A M A 10 10 5 10 5	40	✗
8	4 3 4 5 6 M A M M E 10 5 10 10 20	55	✓
9	3 2 2 1 4 A A A A M 5 5 5 5 10	30	✗
10	5 6 5 1 5 M E M A M 10 20 10 5 10	55	✓
11	1 1 1 3 2 A A A A A 5 5 5 5 5	25	✗
12	3 3 1 5 3 A A A M A 5 5 5 10 5	30	✗
13	6 2 2 4 4 E A A M M 20 5 5 10 10	50	✓
14	6 5 4 1 4 E M M A M 20 10 10 5 10	55	✓
15	5 1 3 1 2 M A A A A 5 5 10 5 5	30	✗
16	3 1 4 3 3 A A M A A 5 5 10 5 5	30	✗
17	3 6 4 4 1 A E M M A 5 20 10 10 5	50	✓
18	6 2 6 5 2 E A E M A 20 5 20 10 5	60	✓
	Totals:	795	9

a Estimate of how much his grandmother will pay him

$= \frac{\text{Total amount of money earned in 18 trials}}{\text{Number of trials}}$

$= \frac{795}{18} = \$44.17$

b Probability that she pays him $50 or more

$= \frac{\text{Total number trials in which \$50 or more was earned}}{\text{Number of trials}}$

$= \frac{9}{18} = 0.5$

4

Trial number	Random numbers and numbers of books	Total number of books	< 30?
1	23 91 83 41 46 96 86 49 43 63 2 5 4 2 3 6 5 3 2 3	35	✗
2	35 68 94 42 4 6 68 90 16 43 2 3 5 2 1 1 3 5 2 2	26	✓
3	27 4 30 72 28 16 67 18 63 88 2 1 2 4 2 2 3 2 3 5	26	✓
4	29 6 51 27 14 27 2 77 98 81 2 1 3 2 2 2 1 4 6 4	27	✓
5	70 51 60 62 21 2 42 87 34 16 3 3 3 3 2 1 2 5 2 2	26	✓
6	12 45 50 69 21 94 79 39 16 61 2 2 3 3 2 5 4 2 2 3	28	✓
7	96 95 79 11 16 6 5 83 57 41 6 5 4 2 2 1 1 4 3 2	30	✗
8	50 54 100 40 73 49 28 46 70 49 3 3 6 2 4 3 2 3 3 3	32	✗
9	8 36 92 80 64 57 21 31 25 71 1 2 5 4 3 3 2 2 2 4	28	✓
10	50 27 51 87 14 69 96 63 97 73 3 2 3 5 2 3 6 3 6 4	37	✗
11	63 54 69 13 21 89 81 5 31 58 3 3 3 2 2 5 4 1 2 3	28	✓
12	72 34 55 78 11 60 95 43 30 11 4 2 3 4 2 3 5 2 2 2	29	✓
13	32 7 76 93 18 69 100 34 26 88 2 1 4 5 2 3 6 2 2 5	32	✗
14	57 45 38 44 30 73 24 77 63 56 3 2 2 2 2 4 2 4 3 3	27	✓
15	9 86 30 83 5 84 29 6 27 96 1 5 2 4 1 4 2 1 2 6	28	✓
16	3 49 58 6 67 95 99 64 9 97 1 3 3 1 3 5 6 3 1 6	32	✗
17	60 58 33 98 38 12 11 99 21 54 3 3 2 6 2 2 2 6 2 3	31	✗
18	93 3 78 20 92 99 26 42 56 38 5 1 4 2 5 6 2 2 3 2	32	✗
19	33 67 61 66 59 32 22 78 96 2 3 3 3 3 3 2 2 4 6 3	31	✗
20	73 37 7 22 3 42 21 78 94 80 4 2 1 2 1 2 2 4 5 4	27	✓
21	63 36 87 96 10 31 49 34 99 34 3 2 5 6 1 2 3 2 6 2	32	✗
22	62 34 96 95 64 38 100 14 10 46 3 2 6 5 3 2 6 2 1 3	33	✗
23	90 55 98 14 7 26 84 77 25 7 5 3 6 2 1 2 4 4 2 1	30	✗
24	38 2 62 75 78 49 21 13 84 28 2 1 3 4 4 3 2 2 4 2	27	✓
25	56 39 91 5 57 55 72 68 35 81 3 2 5 1 3 3 4 3 2 4	30	✗
	Totals:	744	12

a Mean number of number of books taken out by the first 10 borrowers in the day

$= \frac{\text{Total number of books taken out in 25 trials}}{\text{Number of trials}}$

$= \frac{744}{25} = 29.76$

b Probability the first 10 borrowers of the day took out fewer than 30 books

$= \frac{\text{Total number of trials in which fewer than 30 books were taken out}}{\text{Number of trials}}$

$= \frac{12}{25} = 0.48$

4 Discussion and assumptions (pp.42-49)

1 *This mean and the probability are only estimates of their true values. If I had done more than 20 trials, my estimates would probably have been more reliable. If I repeated the simulation, I would almost certainly get different results.*

I have used a die for this simulation, and assumed that it was a fair one. If it was not fair, then the number of ones thrown (correct answers) may have been too high or too low. As a result, my estimates for the mean number of correct answers and the probability of getting five or more correct answers would probably not be very reliable.

It is stated in the question that the person answering the test knows nothing about the topic. However, a common view is that the longer answers in a multi-choice tests are more likely to be correct than the shorter answers. If the person sitting the test knew that, and if the longer answers in the test were more often correct, then the simulation probability for answering

 ISBN: 9780170415996

correctly would be too low. As a result, both the estimated mean number of correct answers and the estimated probability of getting five or more correct would be underestimated by the simulation.

2 *This mean and the probability are only estimates of their true values. If I had done more than 20 trials, my estimates would probably have been more reliable. If I repeated the simulation, I would almost certainly get different results.*

I have assumed that he has estimated the probabilities for single kids, twins and triplets correctly. If he has not, then the probabilities used in the simulation will not be correct, and he will be unlikely to get reliable estimates of the numbers of kids produced or the probability that the flock produces 20 kids or more.

3 *This mean and the probability are only estimates of their true values. If I had done more than 18 trials, my estimates would probably have been more reliable. If I repeated the simulation, I would almost certainly get different results.*

For a simulation to produce reliable estimates, the events must be independent. In this contest it means that the result from one standard does not have any effect on the results for later standards. However, there is a saying that 'success breeds success'. If the first result is a good one, then that inspires confidence and might encourage harder work, so later results tend to be better. In the simulation, the probabilities remained constant. Consequently, if his first result was a good one, both the estimate of how much his grandmother would pay him and the probability that he earns at least $50 might be too low. Conversely, if he did badly in the first test, the estimates might be too high.

At the time he made his estimates for the probabilities, he might not have known about his teacher or his class. If his teacher turned out to be a very good one, or his class was small, he would probably do better than he had estimated. This would mean that the simulation probabilities would be too low. So once again both the estimate of how much his grandmother would pay him and the probability that he earns at least $50 would also be too low. Conversely, if he had a bad teacher or a big class, the estimates might be too high.

4 *This mean and the probability are only estimates of their true values. If I had done more than 25 trials, my estimates would probably have been more reliable. If I repeated the simulation, I would almost certainly get different results.*

I have assumed that the probabilities for the numbers of books taken out by all their customers are the same as those for the first 10 customers in the day. This assumption is likely to be invalid, because people who come to the library early may, for instance, be in a hurry to get somewhere after their library visit, so they may take out fewer books than other customers. If that is the case, then the probabilities used in the simulation for taking out 4, 5 or 6 books would probably be too high. This would mean that estimate of the mean number of books taken out would be higher than the actual mean. The estimated probability that they took out fewer than 30 books in total would be too low.

Practice simulation (pp. 52–56)

1 *The device I will use is a die (or a calculator).*
This is how I will use my device:

- *I will throw a six-sided die and record each number shown.*
- *This means that the probability of getting each of the numbers 1 to 6 is $\frac{1}{6}$.*
- *I will use a 1, 2, 3 or 4 to represent getting a head, thorax, wing or feeler respectively.*
- *If I throw a 5 or a 6, then that represents getting a leg.*

Every possible outcome	Head	Thorax	Wings	Feelers	Legs
Probability of each outcome	$\frac{1}{6}$	$\frac{1}{6}$	$\frac{1}{6}$	$\frac{1}{6}$	$\frac{1}{3}$
Numbers on device	1	2	3	4	5 or 6

2 *One trial consists of throwing the die until I have one head, one thorax, two wings, two feelers and six legs.*
I will do 30 trials.

Example of one trial: I have coloured the useful beetle parts.

Number	1	4	1	4	4	5	3	6	1	4	4	4	5	4	5
Outcome	H	F	H	F	F	L	W	L	H	F	F	F	L	F	L

Number	2	2	5	4	2	6	2	3
Outcome	T	T	L	F	T	L	T	W

Trial outcome: This means that it took 23 turns to complete a beetle, so the beetle was not completed in 20 turns or fewer.

3 You will have to get your teacher to check your simulation and calculations.

4 **Discussion and assumptions:**

This mean and the probability are only estimates of their true values. If I had done more than 25 trials, my estimates would probably have been more reliable. If I repeated the simulation, I would almost certainly get different results.

I have assumed that the die is a fair die, and not loaded to produce more of any one number.

If it is not a fair die, and some numbers are more likely to come up than others, then completing the beetle may take more or fewer turns on average. Legs are most likely to be the last component needed to complete a beetle because there are six needed and the probability of getting legs is less than six times that of getting a head or thorax. So if the die were weighted to produce more or fewer 5s or 6s, then the calculations of the expected number of turns and the probability would not be reliable.

Practice tasks (pp. 57–71)

Examples of answers are given below. For results and calculations for your simulation, you will need to check your answers with your teacher.

Practice task one (pp. 57–61)

1 **Device:**

The device I will use is my graphics calculator.
This is how I will use my device:

- *I will use my calculator with the formula Ran Int# (1, 10). This will produce random numbers from 1 to 10.*
- *I will use the numbers 1 to 10, so the probability of getting each number is 0.1.*

Type of prize	Pie	Drink	Movie ticket
Probability	0.4	0.4	0.2
Random numbers	1 to 4	5 to 8	9 and 10

2 **Trials:**

One trial will consist of finding enough random numbers to produce three movie tokens or 10 tokens, whichever comes first. The maximum number of random numbers in a trial will be 10 because he wants to know how likely it is that he can claim a movie ticket after 10 days.
I will do 30 trials.
Example of one trial:

P = pie, D = drink, M = movie ticket

Day number	1	2	3	4	5	6	7	8	9	10
Random number	1	7	10	3	5	5	5	1	4	6
Outcome	P	D	M	P	D	D	D	P	P	D

Trial outcome: This means that he had to buy six pies, by which time he had three drink tokens so he could claim a free drink. At the end of the trial, he had only one movie token, so he could not claim a free movie ticket after 10 working days.

3 **Results and conclusion:**

You will have to get your teacher to check your simulation and calculations.

4 **Discussion and assumptions:**

My calculations are only estimates of their true values. If I had done more than 30 trials, my estimates would probably have been more reliable. If I repeated the simulation, I would almost certainly get different results.

I have assumed that the probabilities of getting each type of token are reliable. However, if, for instance, the tokens had not been mixed up properly before they were distributed to the retailers, the shop he bought his pies from might have had more or fewer of a particular token type. This would mean that the outcomes of the simulation would not reflect the real situation, so he might be more or less likely to collect three movie tokens.

How the tokens are allocated is not described. If the retailer just hands over a token, he could select which tokens he gave people, or people could ask for particular tokens. This would almost certainly reduce the number of pies that need to be bought before three identical tokens are collected, and make it more likely that he would qualify for a movie ticket within the 10 working days.

Practice task two (pp. 62–67)

Device:

The device I will use is my graphics calculator.
This is how I will use my device:

- *I will use my calculator with the formula Ran Int# (1, 100). This will produce random numbers from 1 to 100.*
- *I will use the numbers 1 to 100, so the probability of getting each number is 0.01.*

Number of people	0	1	2	3	4
Probability	0.06	0.22	0.45	0.09	0.18
Random numbers	1 to 6	7 to 28	29 to 73	74 to 82	83 to 100

ISBN: 9780170415996

Trials:

One trial will consist of finding seven random numbers.
I will do 30 trials.
Example of one trial:

Random number	46	28	98	1	19	26	56
Outcome	2	1	4	0	1	1	2

Trial outcome: This means that one unit had 0 people, three units had 1 person, two units had 2 people and one unit had 4 people. The total number that stayed was 11 people, so his income for that night was 6 x $90 + 11 x $25 = $815, so the motel was not profitable.

Results and conclusion:

You will have to get your teacher to check your simulation and calculations.

Discussion and assumptions:

My calculations are only estimates of their true values. If I had done more than 30 trials, my estimates would probably have been more reliable. If I repeated the simulation, I would almost certainly get different results.

I have assumed that his estimates of the probabilities for the number of people who will occupy his motel during March are reliable. If, for instance, there was a bout of particularly good or bad weather, then it is likely that his probabilities would change. Good weather would probably increase the mean number of people staying each night, and therefore his profitability.

His annual average overall costs for the motel may not reflect the costs for March. For example, if he has a lot of people staying then his labour costs for cleaning, laundry, etc. would probably be higher. So that would mean his profit for March might not be as high as expected.

Practice task three (pp. 68–71)

Device:

The device I will use is my graphics calculator.
This is how I will use my device:

- *I will use my calculator with the formula Ran Int# (1, 100). This will produce random numbers from 1 to 100.*
- *I will use the numbers 1 to 100, so the probability of getting each number is 0.01.*

Gift	Backpack	Umbrella	Sunscreen	Sun hat	Beach towel
Probability	0.21	0.14	0.25	0.08	0.32
Random numbers	1 to 21	22 to 35	36 to 60	61 to 68	69 to 100

One trial will consist of finding 12 random numbers.
I will do 30 trials.
Example of one trial:

b = backpack, u = umbrella, s = sunscreen, h = sun hat, b = beach towel

Random number	*27*	*4*	*30*	*72*	*28*	*16*	*67*	*18*	*63*	*23*	*98*	*88*
Outcome	*u*	*b*	*u*	*t*	*u*	*b*	*h*	*b*	*h*	*u*	*t*	*t*

So three passengers on this cruise asked for backpacks, four asked for umbrellas, none asked for sunscreen, two asked for a hat, and three asked for a towel. That means one of the passengers who asked for an umbrella would not get one because there were only three on board.

You will have to get your teacher to check your simulation and calculations.

Discussion and assumptions:

My calculations are only estimates of their true values. If I had done more than 30 trials, my estimates would probably have been more reliable. If I repeated the simulation, I would almost certainly get different results.

I have assumed that the probabilities of passengers choosing a particular gift are reliable. However, it is likely that these will vary depending on the weather. On a hot, sunny day, more passengers would be likely to ask for sunscreen, sunhats and beach towels, so more of these should be carried and fewer backpacks and umbrellas. If it was raining, then they should carry more umbrellas and fewer bottles of sunscreen, sun hats and towels.